The Varieties of the Meditative Experience

DANIEL GOLEMAN

IRVINGTON PUBLISHERS, Inc., New York

Halsted Press Division of
John Wiley & Sons

New York   London   Toronto   Sydney

Distributed by HALSTED PRESS
A division of JOHN WILEY & SONS, Inc., New York

Reprinted by arrangement with E. P. Dutton, 2 Park Avenue, New York, NY 10016.

Library of Congress Cataloging in Publication Data

Goleman, Daniel.
　The varieties of the meditative experience.

　"A Halsted Press book."
　Bibliography: p.
　Includes index.
　1. Meditation.　I. Title.
BL627.G66 1977b　　291.4'3　　78-539
ISBN 0-470-99191-7

Printed in the United States of America

To Neemkaroli Baba,
for Anasuya, Govinddas, and Hanuman

CONTENTS

FOREWORD

Swiftly arose and spread around me the peace and
joy and knowledge that passes all the art and argu-
ment of the earth; and I know that the hand of God
is the elder hand of my own, and I know that the
Spirit of God is the eldest brother of my own . . .

—Walt Whitman
Leaves of Grass

I have been in that heaven the most illumined
By light from Him, and seen things which to utter
He who returns hath neither skill nor knowledge;
For as it nears the object of its yearning
Our intellect is overwhelmed so deeply
It can never retrace the path that it followed.
But whatsoever of the holy kingdom
Was in the power of memory to treasure
Will be my theme until the song is ended.

—Dante
Inferno

Most of us do not have quite such a vivid and compelling experience as did Dante or Whitman, yet you and I do have moments when we become disoriented in time and/or space; moments when we seem to be at the doorway to another state of being; moments when our own personal viewpoint seems trivial and we sense a greater intuitive harmony in the universe. Perhaps your experiences have come after becoming "lost" in a compelling film, book, piece of art or music, or church service; perhaps after a period of reverie near a brook, a mountain, or the ocean; possibly as the result of a high fever; at the moment of a traumatic event; through drugs or childbirth; from looking at the stars or falling in love. What is so provocative about these moments is that we are out of personal control, and yet all seems harmonious and all right.

In these experiences we sense, though usually cannot articulate, a more profound meaning to our lives. The *sine qua non* of these experiences is that they are not mediated by our intellect. Often, however, immediately after they pass, we return to our analytic minds and attempt to label what has happened. And there is where the trouble begins. Disputes about labels have led to incredible human misunderstandings, even culminating in religious wars. Once we have labeled our experiences, these labels take on power of their own through their association with profound moments and, in addition, they give our egos the security that we know what's what, that we are in control. Some labels treat the experiences as psychological apparition: "I was out of my mind," a "hallucination," a "dissociated state," "surfacing of the unconscious mind," "hysteria," "delusion." Other labels, focusing on the content, imply a mystical or spiritual event: "God came to me"; "I came into the spirit"; "I felt the Presence of Christ," or "a spirit guide"; "I understood the Tao," or "the Dharma," or "the Divine Law."

In 1961 I became involved in a labeling dispute. Having ingested psilocybin, I had the most profound experience of my life to date. The context was religio-mystical, and a spiritual label seemed appropriate. However, I was at the time a social science professor at Harvard, and thus was quite sympathetic to labels that implied that the chemical was a psychotomimetic—that is, it made you crazy. If the chemical didn't make me crazy, I suspected the labeling conflict (often within myself) would ultimately do so. Carl Jung describes the insanity of Richard Wilhelm, translator of the *I Ching*, to be the result of his attempt to incorporate two disparate cultures into his being simultaneously.

Outwardly, the battle revolved around the little psilocybin mushroom. The Mexican Curanderos labeled it *Teonanactyl*—the flesh of the Gods—useful for divinitory and mystical experiences. Humphry Osmond made the labeling a little more palatable for the Western mind by inventing the word *psychedelic*, meaning "mind manifesting." The psychiatric community's label of the same mushroom was "a psychotomimetic triptomine derivative," of interest only for the experimental induction of pseudo-schizophrenic states. Using one labeling system, we were explorers into the mystical realms tried by Moses, Mohammed, Christ, and Buddha. According to the other, we were damn fools, driving ourselves insane.

There was an intuitive validity to the use of the spiritual metaphors. Corroboration for these interpretations came from obvious parallels between the immediate experiences with psychedelics and the mystic literature. I resolved the almost unbearable dissonance by shifting in the direction of a spiritual interpretation. For five years we attempted to find labels that would optimize the value of these experiences for mankind. The issue had significant implications for the politics of human consciousness. Using one set of metaphors, every state of mind not continuous with rational, normal, waking consciousness was to be treated as deviant—as a reflection of lack of adjustment. The other set of metaphors treated altered states of consciousness as rare and precious opportunities for humanity to delve into greater realms of its own potential awareness. As such, these experiences ought to be cultivated rather than suppressed, even if they create a threat to existing social institutions. By raising this issue we were following in the footsteps of William James who, in 1902, wrote of altered states of consciousness in *Varieties of Religious Experience:*

> No account of the universe in its totality can be final, which leaves these other forms of consciousness quite disregarded. How to regard them is the question, for they are so discontinuous with ordinary consciousness. Yet they may determine attitudes, though they cannot furnish formulas, and open a region though they fail to give a map. At any rate, they forbid a premature closing of our accounts with reality.

We came to appreciate the sophistication and sensitivity of Eastern systems of labeling altered states of consciousness. For approximately 4000 years Eastern religions had been evolving maps and charts for the terrain of inner exploration. We could understand some of these, while others were based on cultural perspectives too alien to our own to be useful. In 1967 I went to India because of the attraction of these maps and I wanted to find a way—or perhaps a teacher—through which I could utilize the maps more effectively. I hoped then to be able to stabilize these altered states of consciousness and integrate them with normal everyday life. None of us had been able to do so with psychedelics.

In India I met Neemkaroli Baba, who was far more than I could have hoped for. He lived in the state called sahaj samadhi, in which altered states of consciousness were an integral part of his life. In his presence one had the feeling of boundless space and timelessness, as well as vast love and compassion. Maharaji, as we called him, once ingested a huge dose of psychedelics and, to my complete surprise, nothing happened. If his awareness was not limited to any place, then there was nowhere to go, for he was already here, in all its possibilities.

Seeing one and being one are two different things— and I'd much rather be one than see one. The question was how to effect the transformation from whom I thought I was to whom or what Maharaji was or wasn't. I took everything that came out of Maharaji's mouth as specific instruction, although I wasn't capable of following all of them. But then it got more complicated because he gave conflicting instructions. Now I realized I was confronting a teacher, like a Zen koan, who was not effective so long as one remained bound to the rational. From where I was standing, in my rational, righteous, analytic mind, I couldn't get to where I thought I was going. What to do?

In the presence of Maharaji I experienced my heart opening and felt previously unexperienced waves of ever more consuming love. Perhaps this was the way— drowning in love. But my mind would not be quiet. The social scientist—that skeptic—was not to be drowned without a struggle. Using all the tools, including my sen-

sual desire and intellect, as well as guilt and sense of responsibility, my ego structure fought back. For example,
in the temples in which Maharaji stayed, there were
statues of Hanuman, a monkey-God who had all power
due to his total devotion to God. Hanuman is deeply
loved and honored by Maharaji's devotees. I sat before an
eight-foot cement statue of a monkey, painted red, and I
sang to him and meditated upon him. Every now and
then a voice would observe, "Ah, sitting worshipping a
cement monkey idol. You've really gone over the edge."
This was the inner battle, for which the Bhagavad Gita is
a metaphor.

My Buddhist friends said that the problem was a matter of discipline of mind and, upon questioning, Maharaji
affirmed that if you brought your mind to one-pointedness you would know God. Perhaps that was what I
had to do. So I started to meditate in earnest. The devotional path allowed too much play of mind, and I had to
get tough with myself. In 1971 I began serious meditation practice in Bodh Gaya, where Buddha had been
enlightened. In a series of ten day courses I, along with
about 100 Westerners, was gently guided into Theravadan Buddhist meditation techniques—the ultimate in
simplicity of practice.

During this period I met Anagarika Munindra, a
Therevadan teacher who seemed, in his almost transparent quality, to reflect the mindful, light equanimity to
which the method pointed. I was exhilarated by my first
tastes of a new deep tranquility. I asked to learn more,
and he introduced me to the Visuddhimagga, part of
Buddhism's scholastic tradition. Finally, I, a Western
psychologist, was truly humbled intellectually. For I saw
what *psyche logos* was really about. Here, in this one vol-
ume, was an exquisitely articulated and inclusive cate-

gory system of mental conditions, plus a philosophy and method for extricating your awareness from the tyranny of your own mind. Here was the labeling system I had been looking for since 1961. It was amazingly free of value judgments and thus lent itself to serving as a way of comparing disparate metaphorical systems concerning altered consciousness. I drank the book like a fine brandy.

Though my intellect was delighted by the system underlying the practices, I found myself becoming dry and resistant to the meditation itself. Was this an error in the way I was practicing the method, or was it a clue that this form of spiritual practice was not my way? I happily left Bodh Gaya to fulfill a promise to attend a bhakti celebration and also to find Maharaji, who was my Guru. You may ask why, if Maharaji, a Hindu, is my Guru, I would go to study Buddhist meditation in the first place—rather than stay with him. Well, the answer was that he wouldn't let me stay with him, and he continuously reiterated "*Sub Ek*" (all is one). He spoke at length of Christ and Buddha, and then threw me out. Therefore, when I was away from Maharaji, it did not seem inconsistent to pursue other traditions. For in the method of Guru, all of the other methods fed the process of purification that would allow me to merge with my beloved Maharaji. To merge would be the end of the journey.

When I left Bodh Gaya I had arranged to spend the summer with Munindra in Kosani, a small Himalayan village. At the last minute he could not come, so Dan Goleman and I, and about twenty others, practiced a collection of Buddhist, Hindu, and Christian methods during that summer. In the course of it, in conversation with Dan, I found that he and I held much in common. We were both trained as psychologists; both connected with Harvard; both had the same Guru; and both had an appreciation of Buddhist theory and meditation practice. He was struggling, as I had been, to integrate these disparate parts of our lives.

There were important differences between Dan and me. Among them was the fact that he was motivated to bring what he could, from these experiences and practices, home to the scientific community. I, on the other hand, had long since left academia. Dan could do the intellectual task of integration. His astute scientific mind, his devotion to Maharaji, and his appreciation of the Buddhist tradition ideally prepared him to provide a needed overview of spiritual paths and the states of consciousness they traverse. As you will find in this book, he has done just that.

When I seek to understand what has happened to me, where I am going, or what is becoming of me, then this book delights me. On the other hand, when I meditate upon my guru in my heart, such books as this are irrelevant. Just as you can't make love if you think too much about it, so you can't *be* love if you think too much about it.

Some will be unhappy with this book, feeling that Dan has given short shrift to the subtleties of their particular method of meditation. For example, from my point of view, nothing he has said here has much to do with the quality of grace which comes from my guru to me. But this is not his intent, for his is an impractical view of the unity of paths that holds no special brief for any one of them. Those who consider their path the only way will be especially upset. Here I refer not only to obvious cases, such as Christian fundamentalists or the Krishna Consciousness organization, but to the subtle snobbery that permeates almost all traditions. Apparently each of us, in our insecurity, must feel that his or her way is *the* best way. A more mature perception is that one method is the best way for me, but other paths suit other people. This book exemplifies that open attitude.

Once we get beyond the emotional attachments to our own methods, we will be able to appreciate this work. It is the beginnings of a systematic semantic foundation for appreciating the universality of the spiritual journey, similar to the philosophical foundation set forth by Aldous Huxley in his *Perennial Philosophy*. And, certainly, when we can recognize the commonalities, then we can honor the differences.

RAM DASS

Barre, Massachusetts

PREFACE

I WROTE the major part of this book while living in a tiny Himalayan village during monsoon season, 1971. For the previous several months I had been studying with Indian yogis and swamis, Tibetan lamas, and southern Buddhist laymen and monks. Strange terms and concepts assailed me: "samadhi," "jhana," "turiya," "nirvana," and a host of others used by these teachers to explain their spiritual paths. Each path seemed to be in essence the same as every other path, but each had its own way of explaining how to travel it and what major landmarks to expect.

I was confused. Things first began to jell in my understanding, though, with a remark by Joseph Goldstein, a teacher of insight meditation, at Bodh Gaya. It's simple mathematics, he said: All meditation systems either aim for One or Zero—union with God or emptiness. The path to the One is through concentration on Him, to the Zero is insight into the voidness of one's mind. This was my first guideline for sorting out meditation techniques.

A month or two later I found myself sitting out the monsoon rains in that hilltop village. Five of us had come there to study with a meditation teacher during the rains. He never showed up. Instead, there came a steady trickle of Westerners, sent by my Guru, Neemkaroli Baba, to "be with Ram Dass," one of the five of us there. By the end of monsoon season there had gathered thirty or forty Western pilgrims. Among them were students of virtually every major spiritual tradition: of the various kinds of Indian yogas, of different sects of Tibetan Buddhism, of Sufism, of Christian contemplation, of Zen, of Gurdjieff, of Krishnamurti, and of innumerable individual swamis, gurus, yogis, and babas. Each brought his or her own small treasure of favored books and his trove of private anecdotes. From these literary and personal sources, I sorted out for myself the main similarities and differences among all these meditation paths.

The writings that evolved into this book began as explanations to myself. I needed maps, and each of these traditions had its own to offer. At various times each of these maps has helped me find my way in meditation or made me feel safe in unfamiliar territory. None is complete of itself, for all of them together will fail to explain every facet of any one meditator's experience. Each of us has his own private road to follow, though for periods we may cover well-traveled paths. The maps included here are among the best traveled. These are popular routes but by no means define the whole terrain. This mental territory is mostly unmapped; each of us is an explorer.

Foremost among my debts in writing this book is to Neemkaroli Baba, who inspired me to take seriously my own path. My understanding owes much to conversations and encounters with Ram Dass, Anagarika Munindra, Chogyam Trungpa, Bhagavan Das, Ananda Mayee Ma, Kunu Rinpoche, Krishnamurti, S. N. Goenka,

Swami Muktananda, Nyanaponika Mahathera, Bhikku Nyanajivako, Joseph Goldstein, Herbert Guenther, K. K. Sah, Father Theophane, Yogi Ramagyadas, Charles Reeder, and many others who actively follow these paths themselves. The editors of the *Journal of Transpersonal Psychology* encouraged me to put my work into the form of articles, from which parts of this book are abridged. My travels in Asia were as a Harvard predoctoral fellow and then as a research training fellow of the Social Science Research Council. My wife and children have suffered with me the long hours required to put this book into its final shape. To all those who have helped me, I am deeply grateful.

Daniel Goleman

Woodstock, New York
Guru Poornima Day, 1976

INTRODUCTION

MEDITATION HAS COME to the West in a big way. At this writing, more than a thousand people a day are starting Transcendental Meditation (TM), the largest group in America. An estimated 775,000 people have been instructed in TM. It is telling that "TM" is a registered trademark: Meditation has become big business.

Such forms of meditation offer us something this culture needs but lacks: While we have mastered the environment, we have just begun to tame our inner world. But meditation has been for millenia the path for the person who seeks to go beyond the limiting goals of the everyday world. Ironically, meditation is now touted as the best way to fulfill those everyday goals and live out worldy visions.

In the rush to capture the market of would-be meditators, some organizations have spread distortions about meditation. The notion, for example, that only one kind of meditation can change one for the better, while others cannot, masks the basic sameness of all meditation techniques. I hope to straighten out such confusions by de-

scribing a dozen major meditation techniques, recogniz-
ing genuine differences as well as similarities.

All these meditation traditions promise to change us;
all agree meditation is the path to that change. In the first
section, I describe the specifics of these changes and the
major landmarks of altered states of consciousness along
the way, from the viewpoints of a dozen major traditions.

A word of caution: These states are quite rare. They
never happen to the majority of meditators. Their likeli-
hood increases with one's length of experience in meditation and a host of other factors, such as depth of concentration, purity and stillness of mind, zeal and energy.
The everyday meditative struggles and pleasures of most
of us are not altered states, though they sometimes approach the limits of our ordinary awareness. Those few
among us, however, who have undergone some of these
altered states will find in the second section reassuring
guideposts to events for which our culture knows no safe
context.

A true altered state requires a qualitative break with
the normal range of one's consciousness. The striking experiences that come to most of us during meditation—deep relaxation, intense body pain, or vivid day-
dreams—are not altered states in this sense, just
unusually intense feelings. The so-called "relaxation response," for example, is simply another term for a normal physiological state in which the body is relaxed, re-
storing itself from stress or exertion. This calm state is a
pleasant experience, but it has little to do with the meditative states that transcend the normal limits of sensory
awareness and that are the basis of religious mysticism.

The founder and early followers of every world religion had altered-state experiences. Moses receiving the

Ten Commandments, Jesus' forty-day vigil in the wilderness, Allah's desert visions, and Buddha's enlightenment under the Bo Tree all bespeak extraordinary states of consciousness. These transcendental states inspired churches, monasteries, and orders of monks and have spawned theologies. But too often the institutions and theologies outlive the transmission of the original states that generated them. Without these living experiences, the institutions are pointless, the theologies empty. In my view, the modern crisis of established religions is due to the absence in our age of the personal experience of these transcendental states, the living spirit at the common base of all religions.

The unity of this transcendental experience is veiled by the different names given it by various religions. The "Kingdom of Heaven," the "Other Shore," and the "Pure Land" are all geographical metaphors for this transcendental mental space. As we learn more about states of consciousness, such seeming differences turn out to reflect discrepancies in outlook rather than in the innate nature of the states themselves. Idiosyncracies of belief create false differences. In meditation, as elsewhere, people apply the names they know to what they see. A turn-of-the-century example is R. M. Bucke, who spontaneously entered an altered state while riding home after an evening of reading Whitman's poetry and subsequently saw his experience in terms of "cosmic consciousness." In the present book, by showing clearly the unity of that experience, we can help to reduce the confusion created by the numerous terms.

As an old Zen saying puts it:

From of old there were not two paths. "Those who have arrived" all walked the same road.

THE VARIETIES OF THE
MEDITATIVE EXPERIENCE

PART ONE

THE VISUDDHIMAGGA:
A MAP FOR INNER SPACE

THE CLASSICAL Buddhist *Abhidhamma* is probably the broadest and most detailed traditional psychology of states of consciousness. In the fifth century A.D., the monk Buddhaghosa summarized the portion of Abhidhamma about meditation into the *Visuddhimagga*, the "Path to Purification" (Nanamoli, 1964).* Buddhaghosa explains that the ultimate "purification" should be strictly understood as *nibbana* (sanskrit: *nirvana*), which is an altered state of consciousness.

The Visuddhimagga was for centuries part of an oral textbook of Buddhist philosophy and psychology that aspiring monks memorized verbatim. Because it is so detailed and complete, the Visuddhimagga gives us a comprehensive picture of a single viewpoint regarding meditation. As such, it will give a good background and basis of comparison for understanding other kinds of meditation, the subject matter of Part II. The Visuddhimagga begins with advice on the best surroundings and attitudes

* Full references to these and other books mentioned in the text can be found in the Bibliography.

1

for meditation. It then describes the specific ways the meditator trains his attention and the landmarks he encounters in traversing the meditative path to the nirvanic state. It ends with the psychological consequences for the meditator of his experience of nirvana.*

The Visuddhimagga is a traditional recipe book for meditation, but it does not necessarily tell us about the specific practices of contemporary Theravadan Buddhists. The progression it describes is an ideal type and as such need not conform to the experiences of any given person. But experienced meditators will most certainly recognize familiar landmarks here and there.

1. PREPARATION
FOR MEDITATION

Practice begins with *sila* (virtue or moral purity). This systematic cultivation of virtuous thought, word, and deed focuses the meditator's efforts for the alteration of consciousness in meditation. Unvirtuous thoughts, for example, sexual fantasies or anger, lead to distractedness during meditation. They are a waste of time and energy for the serious meditator. Psychological purification means paring away distracting thoughts.

The purification process is one of three major divisions

---

* In addition to the excellent translation from the original Pali by Bhikku Nanamoli (1976), other contemporary commentaries on the Visuddhimagga consulted include: Bhikku Soma (1949), E. Conze (1956), Kalu Rimpoche (1974), Kashyap (1954), Lama Govinda (1969), Ledi Sayadaw (1965), Mahasi Sayadaw (1965, 1970), Narada Thera (1956), Nyanaponika Thera (1949, 1962, 1968), Nyanatiloka (1952a and b, 1972), P. V. Mahathera (1962).

of training in the Buddhist schema, the other two being *samadhi* (meditative concentration) and *puñña* (insight). Insight is understood in the special sense of "seeing things as they are." Purification, concentration, and insight are closely related. Efforts to purify the mind facilitate initial concentration, which enables sustained insight. By developing either concentration or insight, purity becomes, instead of an act of will, effortless and natural for the meditator. Insight reinforces purity, while aiding concentration; strong concentration can have as by-products both insight and purity. The interaction is not linear; the development of any one facilitates the other two. There is no necessary progression, rather a simultaneous spiral of these three in the course of the meditation path. Though the presentation here is of necessity linear, there is a complex interrelation in the meditator's development of purity, concentration, and insight. These are three facets of a single process.

Active purification in the Visuddhimagga tradition begins with the observance of codes of discipline for laity, novices, and fully ordained monks. The precepts for laity are but five: abstaining from killing, stealing, unlawful sexual intercourse, lying, and intoxicants. For novices the list expands to ten, the first five becoming stricter in the process. For monks there are 227 prohibitions and observances regulating every detail of daily monastic life. While the practice of purity varies with one's mode of life, its intent is the same: It is the necessary preparation for meditation.

On one level these are codes for proper social behavior, but that is secondary in importance to the motivational purity that proper behavior foreshadows. Purity is understood not only in the ordinary external sense of propriety but also as the mental attitudes out of which proper speech, action, and thought arise. Thus, for example, the Visuddhimagga urges the meditator, should lustful thoughts arise, immediately to counter those thoughts by contemplating the body in the aspect of loathsomeness. The object is to free the meditator from thoughts of remorse, guilt, or shame, as well as from lust. Behavior is controlled because it affects the mind. Acts of purity are meant to produce a calmed and subdued mind. The purity of morality has only the purity of mind as its goal.

Because a controlled mind is the goal of purity, restraint of the senses is part of purification. The means for this is *sati* (mindfulness). In mindfulness, control of the senses comes through cultivating the habit of simply noticing sensory perceptions, not allowing them to stimulate the mind into thought chains of reaction. Mindfulness is the attitude of paying sensory stimuli only the barest attention. When systematically developed into the practice of *vipassana* (seeing things as they are), mindfulness becomes the avenue to the nirvanic state. In daily practice, mindfulness leads to detachment toward the meditator's own perceptions and thoughts. He becomes an onlooker to his stream of consciousness, weakening the pull to normal mental activity and so preparing the way to altered states.

In the initial stages, before firm grounding in mindfulness, the meditator is distracted by his surroundings. The Visuddhimagga accordingly gives instructions to the would-be meditator for the optimum life style and setting. He must engage in "right livelihood" so that the source of his financial support will not be cause for misgivings; in the case of monks, professions such as astrology, palm reading, and dream interpretation are expressly forbidden, while the life of a mendicant is recommended. Possessions should be kept to a minimum; a monk is to possess only eight articles: three robes, a belt, a begging bowl, a razor, a sewing needle, and sandals. He should take food in moderation, enough to ensure physical health but less than would make for drowsiness. His dwelling should be aloof from the world, a place of solitude; for householders who cannot live in isolation, a room should be set aside for meditation. Undue concern for the body should be avoided, but in case of sickness, the meditator should obtain appropriate medicine. In acquiring the four requisites of possessions, food, dwelling, and medicine, the meditator should get only what is necessary to his well-being. In getting these requisites, he should act without greed, so that even his material necessities will be untainted by impurity.

Since one's own state of mind is affected by the state of mind of one's associates, the serious meditator should surround himself with likeminded people. This is one advantage of a *sangha*, narrowly defined as those who have attained the nirvanic state and, in its widest sense, the community of people on the path. Meditation is helped by the company of mindful or concentrated persons and is harmed by those who are agitated, distracted, and immersed in worldly concerns. Agitated, worldly people are likely to talk in a way that does not lead to detachment, dispassion, or tranquility, qualities the meditator seeks to cultivate. The sort of topics typical of worldly, unprofitable talk are enumerated by the Buddha as (Nyanaponika Thera, 1962: p. 172):

> . . . about kings, thieves, ministers, armies, famine, and war; about eating, drinking, clothing and lodging; about garlands, perfumes, relatives, vehicles, cities and countries; about women and wine, the

gossip of the street and well; about ancestors and various trifles; tales about the origin of the world, talk about things being so or otherwise, and similar matters.

At later stages, the meditator may find to be obstacles what once were aids. The Visuddhimagga lists ten categories of potential attachments, all hindrances to progress in meditation: (1) any fixed dwelling place if its upkeep is the cause of worry, (2) family, if their welfare causes concern, (3) accruing gifts or reputation that involves spending time with admirers, (4) a following of students or being busy with teaching, (5) projects, having "something to do," (6) traveling about, (7) people dear to one whose needs demand attention, (8) illness necessitating undergoing treatment, (9) theoretical studies unaccompanied by practice, and (10) supernormal psychic powers, the practice of which becomes more interesting than meditation. Release from these obligations frees the meditator for single-minded pursuit of meditation: This is "purification" in the sense of freeing the mind from worrisome matters. The life of the monk is designed for this kind of freedom; for the layman, short retreats allow a temporary reprieve.

These ascetic practices are optional in the "middle way" of the Buddha. The serious monk can practice them, should he find any of them helpful. But he must be discreet in their observance, doing them so that they will not attract undue attention. These practices include wearing only robes made of rags; eating only one bowl of food, and just once a day; living in the forest under a tree; dwelling in a cemetery or in the open; sitting up throughout the night. Though optional, the Buddha praises those who follow these modes of living "for the sake of frugality, contentedness, austerity, detachment," while criticizing those who pride themselves on practicing austerities and look down on others who do not. In all facets of training, spiritual pride mars purity. Any gains from asceticism are lost in pride. The goal of purification is simply a mind unconcerned with externals, calm and ripe for meditation.

Entering the Path of Concentration

Purity is the psychological base for concentration. The essence of concentration is nondistractedness; purification is the systematic pruning away of sources of distraction. Now the meditator's work is to attain unification of mind, one-pointedness. The stream of thought is normally random and scattered. The goal of concentration in meditation is to focus the thought flow by fixing the mind on a single object, the meditation topic. In the later stages of concentrative meditation, the mind is not only directed toward the object but finally penetrates it; totally absorbed in it, the mind moves to oneness with the object. When this happens, the object is the only thing in the meditator's awareness.

Any object of attention can be the subject for concentrative meditation, which is simply sustaining a single point of focus. But the character of the object attended to has definite consequences for the outcome of meditation. The Visuddhimagga recommends forty meditation subjects:

—ten *kasinas:* colored wheels about a foot in circumference: earth, water, fire, air, dark blue, yellow, blood-red, white, light, bounded space

—ten *asubhas:* loathsome, decaying corpses; for example, a bloated corpse, a gnawed corpse, a
  worm-infected corpse, etc., including a skeleton
—ten reflections: on the attributes of the Buddha,
  the Doctrine, the sangha, peace, one's own purity, one's own liberality, one's own possessions of
  godly qualities, or on the inevitability of death;
  contemplation on the thirty-two parts of the body
  or on in-and-out breathing
—four sublime states: loving-kindness, compassion,
  joy in the joy of others, and equanimity
—four formless contemplations: of infinite space, infinite consciousness, the realm of nothingness, and
  the realm of "neither perception nor non perception"; the loathsomeness of food
—the four physical elements: earth, air, fire, water
  as abstract forces (i.e., extension, motility, heat,
  cohesion)

Each of these subjects has specific consequences for the
nature, depth, and by-products of concentration; meditation on a corpse, for example, becomes very different
from contemplating loving-kindness. All of these subjects
are suitable for developing concentration to the depth
necessary for attaining the nirvanic state. The concentration produced by those of a complicated nature—for example, the attributes of the Buddha—is less unified than
that produced by a simple object—for example, the earth
kasina, a clay-colored wheel. Apart from the depth of
concentration produced by a given meditation subject,
each has distinct psychological by-products. The meditation on loving-kindness, for example, has several results:
The meditator sleeps and wakes in comfort; he dreams
no evil dreams; he is dear to all beings; his mind is easily

concentrated; his expression is serene; and he dies unconfused.

The Buddha saw that persons of different temperaments are more suited to some meditation subjects than to others. His guidelines for matching people to the best meditation subject is based on these main types of temperament: (1) one disposed to hatred; (2) the lustful, deluded, or excitable; (3) one prone to faith; (4) the intelligent.

Subjects suitable for the hateful type are: the four sublime states and the four color kasinas; for the lustful, the ten corpses, the body parts, and the breath; for the faithful, the first six reflections; and for the intelligent, reflection on death, the loathsomeness of food, and the physical elements. The remaining subjects are suitable for everyone. The Visuddhimagga also specifies the appropriate physical surrounding for each type. The lustful meditator, for example, should be assigned a cramped, windowless hut in an ugly location in the neighborhood of unfriendly people; the hateful type, on the other hand, is to be given a comfortable and roomy cottage in a pleasant area near helpful people.

The Teacher

The ideal meditation teacher was the Buddha, who, it is said, had developed the power to know the mind and heart of others. He perfectly matched each person with the appropriate subject and circumstance for concentration. In lieu of such an ideal teacher, the Visuddhimagga advises the would-be meditator to pick his * teacher ac-

---

* For "he" and "him" throughout this book, read "he/she" and "him/her." The path of meditation is clearly not closed to members of any sex, race, or creed.

cording to level of attainment in meditation, the most highly accomplished being the best teacher. The teacher's support and advice are critical to the meditator in making his way through unfamiliar mental terrain. The pupil "takes refuge" in his teacher, entering a contract of surrender to him.

The pupil surrenders egoism, the source of hindrances that prevent him from pursuing meditation to the point at which egoism is transcended. But the responsibility for salvation is laid squarely on the student's own shoulders, not on the teacher's; the teacher is merely a "good friend" on the path. The teacher points the way; the student must walk for himself. The essence of the teacher's role is given in the lines from the Japanese *Zenrin:*

If you wish to know the road up the mountain,
You must ask the man who goes back and forth
    on it.

2. THE PATH
OF CONCENTRATION

In describing the path of concentration, the Visuddhimagga map suffers from a serious oversight: It begins with the description of an advanced altered state, one that many or most meditators may never once experience. It skips the ordinary—and much more common— preliminary stages. This gap can be filled from other Buddhist sources, which start with the meditator's normal state of mind rather than with the rarefied states the Visuddhimagga elaborates in detail.

At the outset, the meditator's focus wanders from the object of meditation. As he notices he has wandered, he returns his awareness to the proper focus. His one-pointedness is occasional, coming in fits and starts. His mind oscillates between the object of meditation and distracting thoughts, feelings, and sensations. The first landmark in concentration comes when the meditator's mind is unaffected both by outer distractions, such as nearby sounds, and by the turbulence of his own assorted thoughts and feelings. Although sounds are heard, and his thoughts and feelings are noticed, they do not disturb the meditator.

In the next stage, his mind focuses on the object for prolonged periods. The meditator gets better at repeatedly returning his mind to the object as it wanders. His ability to return his attention gradually increases as the meditator sees the ill results of distractions (e.g., agitation) and feels the advantages of a calm one-pointedness. As this happens, the meditator is able to overcome mental habits antagonistic to calm collectedness, such as boredom due to hunger for novelty. By now, the meditator's mind can remain undistracted for long periods.

On the Verge of Absorption

In the early stages of meditation, there is a tension between concentration on the object of meditation and distracting thoughts. The main distractions are sensual desires; ill will, despair, and anger; sloth and torpor; agitation and worry; and doubt and skepticism. With much practice, a moment comes when these hindrances

are wholly subdued. There is then a noticeable quicken-
ing of concentration. At this moment, the mental attributes, such as one-pointedness and bliss, that will mature
into full absorption simultaneously come into dominance.
Each has been present previously to different degrees,
but when they come, all at once they have special power.
This is the first noteworthy attainment in concentrative
meditation; because it is the state verging on full absorption, it is called "access" concentration.

This state of concentration is like a child not yet able
to stand steady but always trying to do so. The mental
factors of full absorption are not strong at the access
level; their emergence is precarious, and the mind fluctu-
ates between them and its inner speech, the usual rumi-
nations and wandering thoughts. The meditator is still
open to his senses and remains aware of surrounding
noises and his body's feelings. The meditation subject is
a dominant thought but does not yet fully occupy the
mind. At this access level, strong feelings of zest or rapture emerge, along with happiness, pleasure, and equanimity. There is also fleeting attention to the meditation
subject as though striking at it, or more sustained focus
on it, repeatedly noting it. Sometimes there are luminous
shapes or flashes of bright light, especially if the meditation subject is a kasina or respiration. There may also be
a sensation of lightness, as though the body were floating
in the air. Access concentration is a precarious attainment. If not solidified into fuller absorption at the same
sitting, it must be protected between sessions by avoiding distracting actions or encounters.

Visions

Visionary experiences can occur on the threshold of this level when factors such as rapture have ripened but discursive thought continues, and so long as sustained focus on the object of concentration remains weak. Were sustained concentration to achieve full strength, mental processes necessary for visions would be cut short as long as attention remains with the primary object. Access and deeper levels of absorption are for this reason antithetical to visions, but as the access level is approached (or on emerging from deeper absorption), visions are most likely. Visions can be frightening—an image of oneself as a corpse, for example, or the form of a threatening and terrifying beast—or quite benign, such as the figure of a benevolent deity or a Buddha. Meditative visions are quite vivid; the Visuddhimagga says they are as realistic as talking to a guest who comes on a visit. Timid or anxious persons who have a terrifying vision, it is warned, can be driven mad. Another danger to the meditator is becoming enraptured by beatific visions and so halting further progress by making them the goal of one's meditation, failing to further strengthen concentration. The meditator's goal is beyond visions. In Zen, they say, "If you meet the Buddha, slay him."

Full Absorptions or Jhana

By continually focusing on the object of meditation, there comes the first moment marking a total break with normal consciousness. This is full absorption, or *jhana*. The mind suddenly seems to sink into the object and remains fixed in it. Hindering thoughts cease totally.

There is neither sensory perception nor the usual awareness of one's body; bodily pain cannot be felt. Apart from the initial and sustained attention to the primary object, consciousness is dominated by rapture, bliss, and one-pointedness. These are the mental factors that, when in simultaneous ascendance, constitute jhana.

There is a subtle distinction between rapture and bliss. Rapture at the level of the first jhana is likened to the initial pleasure and excitement of getting a long-sought object; bliss is the enjoyment of that object. Rapture may be experienced as raising of the hairs on the body, as momentary joy that flashes and disappears like lightning, as waves showering through the body again and again, as the sensation of levitation, or as immersion in thrilling happiness. Bliss is a more subdued state of continued ecstasy. One-pointedness is the property of mind that centers it in the jhanic state. The first taste of jhana lasts but a single moment, but with continued efforts, the jhanic state can be held for longer and longer intervals. Until the jhana is mastered, it is unstable and can be easily lost. Full mastery comes when the meditator can attain jhana whenever, wherever, as soon as, and for as long as he wishes.

Deeper Jhanas

In the course of meditation, one-pointedness becomes more and more intensified by the successive elimination of the jhanic factors. One-pointedness absorbs the energy invested in the other factors at each deeper jhanic level (Fig. 1). Becoming even more one-pointed after mastery of the first jhana requires eliminating initial and repeated returning of the mind to the meditation object. After

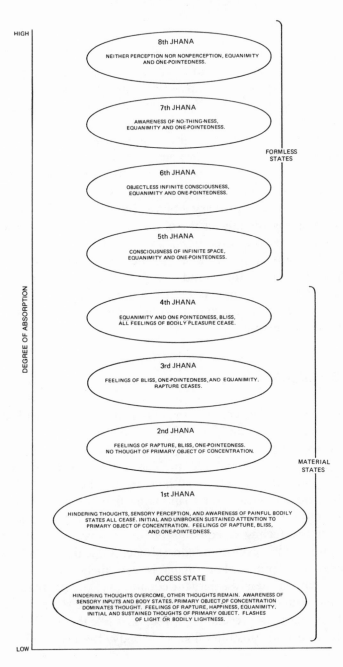

Fig. 1. Landmarks on the Path of Concentration.

emerging from the jhanic state, these attentional processes seem gross in comparison to the other more subtle
mental factors of jhana. Just as the hindrances were overcome on the way to the access level, and just as thoughts
were stilled in attaining the first jhana, initial and repeated attention to the primary object are abandoned at
the threshold of the second jhana. To go beyond these
kinds of attention, the meditator enters the first jhana by
focusing on the primary object. But then he frees the
mind of any thought of the object by instead turning the
mind toward rapture, bliss, and one-pointedness. This
level of absorption is more subtle and stable than the
first. The meditator's mind is now totally free of any verbal thoughts, even that of the original primary object.
Only a reflected image of the object remains as the focus
of one-pointedness.

Third Jhana

To go still deeper, the meditator masters the second
jhana as he did the first. Then, when he emerges from
the second jhana, he sees that rapture—a form of excitement—is gross compared to bliss and one-pointedness.
He attains the third level of jhana by again contemplating
the primary object and abandoning first thoughts of the
object, then rapture. In the third level of absorption,
there is a feeling of equanimity toward even the highest
rapture. This even-mindedness emerges with the fading
away of rapture. This jhana is extremely subtle, and
without this newly emergent equanimity, the meditator's
mind would be pulled back to rapture. If he stays in the
third jhana, an exceedingly sweet bliss fills the meditator,
and afterward this bliss floods his body. Because the bliss

of this level is accompanied by equanimity, the meditator's mind is kept one-pointed in these subtle dimensions, resisting the pull of a grosser rapture. Having mastered the third jhana as those before, the meditator can go deeper if he sees that bliss is more disturbing than one-pointedness and equanimity.

Fourth Jhana

To go deeper still, the meditator has to abandon all forms of mental pleasure. He has to give up all those mental states that might oppose more total stillness, even bliss and rapture. With the total cessation of bliss, equanimity and one-pointedness gain their full strength. In the fourth jhana, feelings of bodily pleasure are fully abandoned; feelings of pain ceased at the first jhana. There is not a single sensation or thought. The meditator's mind at this extremely subtle level rests with one-pointedness in equanimity. Just as his mind becomes progressively more still at each level of absorption, his breath becomes calmer. At this fourth level, the meditator's breath is so still he cannot sense the least stirring; he perceives his breath as ceasing altogether.

Formless Jhana

The next step in concentration culminates in the four states called "formless." The first four jhanas are attained by concentration on a material form or some concept derived therefrom. But the meditator attains the formless states by passing beyond all perception of form. To enter the first four jhanas, the meditator had to empty his mind of mental factors. To enter each successive formless jhana, the meditator substitutes progressively more subtle objects of concentration. All the formless jhanas share the mental factors of one-pointedness and equanimity, but at each level these factors are more refined. Concentration approaches imperturbability. The meditator cannot be disturbed but emerges after a self-determined time limit set before entering this state.

Fifth Jhana

The meditator reaches the first formless absorption and the fifth jhana by entering the fourth jhana through any of the kasinas. Mentally extending the limits of the kasina to the largest extent imaginable, his attention is then turned away from the colored light of the kasina and toward the space occupied by it. With this infinite space as the object of contemplation and with the full maturity of equanimity and one-pointedness, the meditator's mind now abides in a sphere in which all perceptions of form have ceased. His mind is so firmly set in this sublime consciousness that nothing can disrupt it. Still, the barest trace of the senses exists in the fifth jhana, though they are ignored. The absorption would be broken should the meditator turn his attention to them.

Once the fifth jhana is mastered, the meditator goes still deeper by first achieving an awareness of infinite space and then turning his attention to that infinite awareness. In this way, the thought of infinite space is abandoned, while objectless infinite awareness remains. This marks the sixth jhana. Having mastered the sixth, the meditator obtains the seventh jhana by first entering the sixth and then turning his awareness to the nonexistence of infinite consciousness. Thus, the seventh jhana is absorption with no-thing-ness, or the void, as its object. That is, the meditator's mind takes as its object the awareness of absence of any object.

Mastering this seventh jhana, the meditator can then review it and find any perception at all a disadvantage, its absence being more sublime. So motivated, the meditator attains the eighth jhana by first entering the seventh. He then turns his attention to the aspect of peacefulness and away from perception of the void. The delicacy of this is suggested by the stipulation that there must be no hint of desire to attain this peacefulness or to avoid perception of no-thing-ness. Attending to the peacefulness, he reaches an ultrasubtle state in which there are only residual mental processes. There is no gross perception here at all: This is a state of "no perception." There *is* ultrasubtle perception: thus, "not nonperception." The eighth jhana, therefore, is called the "sphere of neither perception nor nonperception." No mental states are decisively present: Their residuals remain, though they are nearly absent. This state approaches the ultimate limits of perception. As with mind, so with body; the meditator's metabolism becomes progressively stiller through the formless jhanas. "The eighth jhana," says one commentator, "is a state so extremely subtle that it cannot be said whether it is or is not."

Each jhana rests on the one below. In entering any jhana, the meditator's mind traverses upward each level in succession by eliminating the gross elements of each one by one. With practice, the traversal of jhanic levels becomes almost instantaneous, the meditator's awareness pausing at each level on the way for but a few moments of consciousness. As grosser mental factors are eliminated, concentration intensifies. The grossness of a meditation subject limits the depth of jhana the meditator can reach through it. The simpler the subject, the deeper the jhana (Table 1).

TABLE 1
JHANA LEVEL ATTAINABLE ACCORDING TO
MEDITATION SUBJECT

	Highest Jhana Level Attainable
Reflections; elements; loathsomeness of food	Access
Body parts; corpses	First
Loving-kindness; selfless joy; compassion	Third
Equanimity	Fourth
Infinite space	Fifth
Infinite consciousness	Sixth
No-thing-ness	Seventh
Kasinas; mindfulness of breath; neither perception nor nonperception	Eighth

3. THE PATH OF INSIGHT

The Visuddhimagga sees mastery of the jhanas and tasting their sublime bliss as of secondary importance to puñña, discriminating wisdom. Jhana mastery is part of a fully rounded training, but its advantages for the meditator are in making his mind wieldy and pliable, so speeding his training in puñña. Indeed, the deeper jhanas are sometimes referred to in Pali, the language of the Visudhimagga, as "concentration games," the play of well-advanced meditators. But the crux of his training is a path that need not include the jhanas. This path begins with mindfulness (*satipatthana*), proceeds through insight (vipassana), and ends in nirvana.

Mindfulness

The first phase, mindfulness, entails breaking through stereotyped perception. Our natural tendency is to become habituated to the world around us, no longer to notice the familiar. We also substitute abstract names or preconceptions for the raw evidence of our senses. In mindfulness, the meditator methodically faces the bare facts of his experience, seeing each event as though occurring for the first time. He does this by continuous attention to the first phase of perception, when his mind is *receptive* rather than reactive. He restricts his attention to the bare notice of his senses and thoughts. He attends to these as they arise in any of the five senses or in his mind, which, in the Visuddhimagga, constitutes a sixth sense. While attending to his sense impressions, the meditator keeps reaction simply to registering whatever he observes. If any further comment, judgment, or reflection arises in the meditator's mind, these are themselves made the focus of bare attention. They are neither repudiated nor pursued but simply dismissed after being noted. The essence of mindfulness is, in the words of Nyanaponika Thera, a modern Buddhist monk, "the clear and single-minded awareness of what actually happens *to* us and *in* us, at the successive moments of perception."

Whatever power of concentration the meditator has developed previously helps him in the thorough pursuit of mindfulness. One-pointedness is essential in adopting this new habit of bare perception. The best level of jhana for practicing mindfulness is the lowest, that of access. This is because mindfulness is applied to normal consciousness, and from the first jhana on, these normal processes cease. A level of concentration less than that of access, on the other hand, can be easily overshadowed by wandering thoughts and lapses in mindfulness. At the access level, there is a desirable balance: Perception and thought retain their usual patterns, but concentration is powerful enough to keep the meditator's awareness being diverted from steadily noting these patterns. The moments of entry to or exit from jhana are especially ripe for practicing insight. The mind's workings are transparent in these moments, making them more vulnerable to the clear gaze of the mindful meditator.

The preferred method for cultivating mindfulness is to precede it with training in the jhanas. There is, however, a method called "bare insight" in which the meditator begins mindfulness without any previous success in concentration. In bare insight, concentration strengthens through the practice of mindfulness itself. During the first stages of bare insight, the meditator's mind is intermittently interrupted by wandering thoughts between moments of mindful noticing. Sometimes the meditator notices the wandering, sometimes not. But momentary concentration gradually strengthens as more stray thoughts are noted. Wandering thoughts subside as soon as noticed, and the meditator resumes mindfulness immediately afterward. Finally, the meditator reaches the point at which his mind is unhindered by straying. When he notices every movement of the mind without break, this is the same as access concentration.

Kinds of Mindfulness

There are four kinds of mindfulness, identical in function but different in focus. Mindfulness can focus on the body, on feelings, on the mind, or on mind objects. Any one of these serves as a fixed point for bare attention to the stream of consciousness. In mindfulness of the body, the meditator attends to each moment of his bodily activity, such as his posture and the movements of his limbs. The meditator notes his body's motion and position regardless of what he does. The aims of his act are disregarded; the focus is on the bodily act itself. In mindfulness of feeling, the meditator focuses on his internal sensations, disregarding whether they are pleasant or unpleasant. He simply notes all his internal feelings as they come to his attention. Some feelings are the first reaction to messages from the senses, some are physical feelings accompanying psychological states, some are by-products of biological processes. Whatever the source, the feeling itself is registered.

In mindfulness of mental states, the meditator focuses on each state as it comes to awareness. Whatever mood, mode of thought, or psychological state presents itself, he simply registers it as such. If, for instance, there is anger at a disturbing noise, at that moment he simply notes "anger." The fourth technique, mindfulness of mind objects, is virtually the same as the one just described save for the level at which the mind's workings are observed. Rather than noting the quality of mental states as they arise, the meditator notes the attentional objects that occupy those states, for example, "disturbing noise." As each thought arises, the meditator notes it in terms of a detailed schema for classifying mental content. The broadest category on this list labels all thoughts as either hindrances to or helps toward enlightenment.

Any of these techniques of mindfulness will break through the illusions of continuity and reasonableness that sustain our mental life. In mindfulness, the meditator begins to witness the random units of mind stuff from which his reality is built. From these observations emerge a series of realizations about the nature of the mind. With these realizations, mindfulness matures into insight. The practice of insight begins at the point when mindfulness continues without lag. In insight meditation, awareness fixes on its object so that the contemplating mind and its object arise together in unbroken succession. This point marks the beginning of a chain of insights—mind knowing itself—ending in the nirvanic state (Fig. 2).

The first realization in insight is that the phenomena contemplated are distinct from mind contemplating them: Within the mind, the faculty whereby mind witnesses its own workings is different from the workings it witnesses. The meditator knows awareness is distinct from the objects it takes, but this knowledge is not at the verbal level as it is expressed here. Rather, the meditator knows this and each ensuing realization in his direct experience. He may have no words for his realizations; he understands but cannot necessarily state that understanding.

Continuing his practice of insight, after the meditator has realized the separate nature of awareness and its objects, he can, with further insight, gain a clear under-

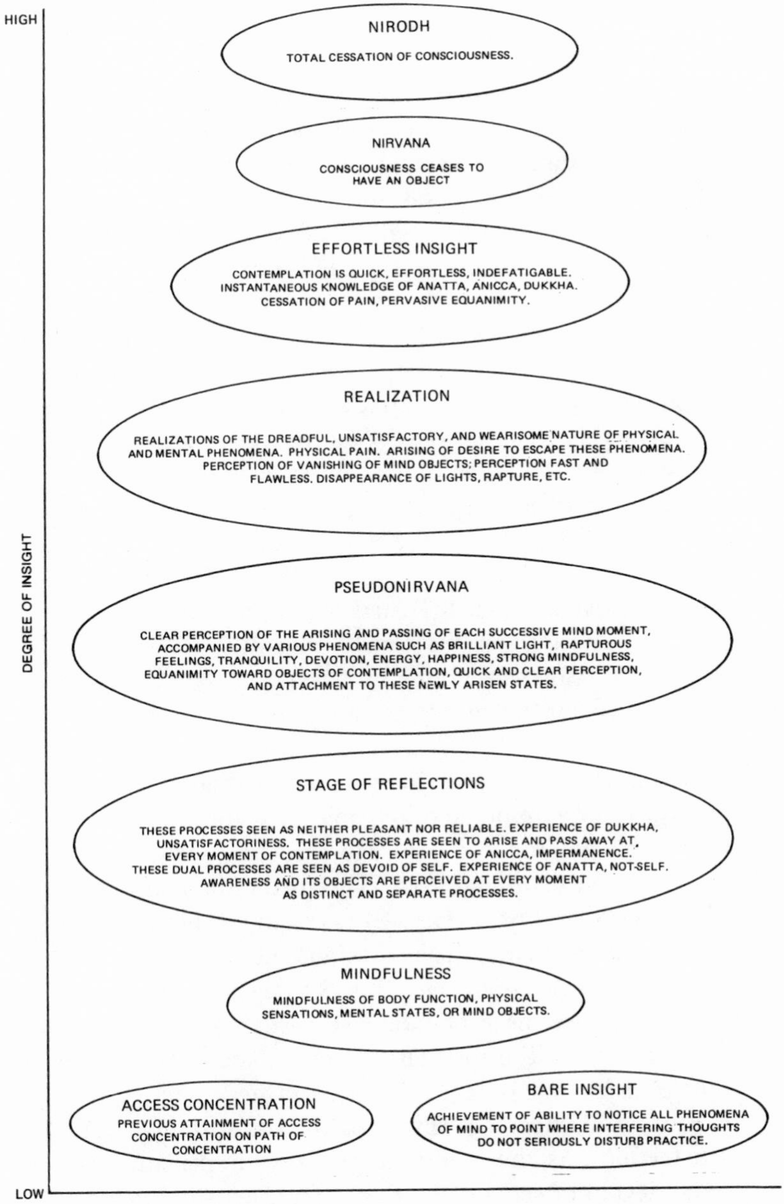

Fig. 2. Landmarks on the Path of Insight.

standing that these dual processes are devoid of self. He sees that they arise as effects of their respective causes, not as the result of direction by any individual agent. Each moment of awareness goes according to its own nature, regardless of "one's will." It becomes certain to the meditator that nowhere in the mind can any abiding entity be detected. This is direct experience of the Buddhist doctrine of *anatta*, literally "not self," that all phenomena have no indwelling personality. This includes even "one's self." The meditator sees his past and future life as merely a conditioned cause-effect process. He no longer doubts whether the "I" really exists; he knows "I am" to be a misconception. He realizes the truth of the words of the Buddha in the Pali Canon:

> Just as when the parts are set together
> There arises the word "chariot,"
> So does the notion of a being
> When the aggregates are present.

Continuing to practice insight, the meditator finds that his witnessing mind and its objects come and go at a frequency beyond his ken. He sees his whole field of awareness in continual flux. The meditator realizes that his world of reality is renewed every mind moment in an endless chain. With this realization, he knows the truth of impermanence (Pali: *anicca*) in the depths of his being.

Finding that these phenomena arise and pass away at every moment, the meditator comes to see them as neither pleasant nor reliable. Disenchantment sets in: What is constantly changing cannot be the basis for any lasting satisfaction. As the meditator realizes his private reality to be devoid of self and ever changing, he is led to a state of detachment from his world of experience. From this detached perspective, the impermanent and impersonal qualities of his mind lead him to see it as a source of suffering (Pali: *dukkha*).

Pseudonirvana

The meditator then continues without any further reflections. After these realizations, the meditator begins to see clearly the beginning and end of each successive moment of awareness. With this clarity of perception, there may occur:

—the vision of a *brilliant light* or luminous form

—*rapturous feelings* that cause goose flesh, tremor in the limbs, the sensation of levitation, and the other attributes of rapture

—*tranquility* in mind and body, making them light, plastic, and wieldy

—*devotional feelings* toward and faith in the meditation teacher, the Buddha, his teachings—including the method of insight itself—and the sangha, accompanied by joyous confidence in the virtues of meditation and the desire to advise friends and relatives to practice it

—*vigor* in meditating, with a steady energy neither too lax nor too tense

—sublime *happiness* suffusing the meditator's body, an unprecedented bliss that seems never-ending and motivates him to tell others of this extraordinary experience

—*quick and clear perception* of each moment of awareness: Noticing is keen, strong, and lucid, and the characteristics of impermanence, nonself, and unsatisfactoriness are clearly understood at once.

—*strong mindfulness* so the meditator effortlessly notices every successive moment of awareness; mindfulness gains a momentum of its own

—*equanimity* toward whatever comes into awareness: No matter what comes into his mind, the meditator maintains a detached neutrality.

—a subtle *attachment* to the lights and other factors listed here and pleasure in their contemplation

The meditator is often elated at the emergence of these ten signs and may speak of them thinking he has attained enlightenment and finished the task of meditation. Even if he does not think they mark his liberation, he may pause to bask in their enjoyment. For this reason, this stage, called "Knowledge of Arising and Passing Away," is subtitled in the Visuddhimagga "The Ten Corruptions of Insight." It is a pseudonirvana. The great danger for the meditator is in "mistaking what is not the Path for the Path" or, in lieu of that, faltering in the further pursuit of insight because of his attachment to these phenomena. Finally, the meditator, either on his own or through advice from his teacher, realizes these experiences to be a landmark along the way rather than his final destination. At this point, he turns the focus of insight on them and on his own attachment to them.

Higher Realizations

As this pseudonirvana gradually diminishes, the meditator's perception of each moment of awareness becomes clearer. He can make increasingly fine discrimination of successive moments until his perception is flawless. As his perception quickens, the ending of each moment of awareness is more clearly perceived than its arising. Finally, the meditator perceives each moment only as it vanishes. He experiences contemplating mind and its object as vanishing in pairs at every moment. The meditator's world of reality is in a constant state of dissolution. A dreadful realization flows from this; the mind becomes gripped with fear. All his thoughts seem fearsome. He sees becoming, that is, thoughts coming into being, as a source of terror. To the meditator everything that enters his awareness—even what might once have been very pleasant—now seems oppressive. He is helpless to avoid this oppression; it is part of every moment.

At this point, the meditator realizes the unsatisfactory quality of all phenomena. The slightest awareness he sees as utterly destitute of any possible satisfaction. In them is nothing but danger. The meditator comes to feel that in all the kinds of becoming there is not a single thing that he can place his hopes in or hold onto. All of his awareness, every thought, every feeling, appears insipid. This includes any state of mind the meditator can conceive. In all the meditator perceives, he sees only suffering and misery.

Feeling this misery in all phenomena, the meditator becomes entirely disgusted with them. Though he continues with the practice of insight, his mind is dominated by feelings of discontent and listlessness toward all its own contents. Even the thought of the happiest sort of life or the most desirable objects seem unattractive and boring. He becomes absolutely dispassionate and adverse toward the multitude of mental stuff—to any kind of becoming, destiny, or state of consciousness.

Between the moments of noticing, it occurs to the meditator that only in the ceasing of all mental processes is relief possible. Now his mind no longer fastens on to its contents, and the meditator desires to escape from the suffering due to these phenomena. Painful feelings may flood his body, and he may no longer be able to remain long in one posture. The comfortless nature of mind stuff becomes more evident than ever; the desire for deliverance from it emerges at the root of his being.

With this strong desire for surcease from mental processes, the meditator intensifies his efforts to notice these processes for the very purpose of escaping them. Their nature—their impermanence, the element of suffering, and their voidness of self—become clearly evident. The meditator's body will sometimes undergo severe, sharp pains of growing intensity. His whole body and mind may seem a mass of suffering; restlessness may overwhelm his insight. But by systematically noting these pains, they will cease. At this point, the meditator's ability at simply noticing becomes strong and lucid. At every moment, he knows quite clearly the three characteristics of mental phenomena. One of these three comes to dominate his understanding.

Now the meditator's contemplation proceeds automatically, without special effort, as if borne onward of itself. Feelings of dread, despair, and misery cease. Body pains are absent entirely. The meditator's mind has abandoned both dread and delight. An exceedingly sublime clarity of mind and a pervasive equanimity emerge. The meditator need make no further deliberate effort; noticing continues in a steady flow for hours without his tiring. His meditation has its own momentum, and insight becomes especially quick.

Insight is now on the verge of its culmination; the meditator's noticing of each moment of awareness is keen, strong, and lucid. The meditator instantly knows each moment to be impermanent, painful, or without self as he sees its dissolution. He sees all mental phenomena as limited and circumscribed, devoid of desirability, or alien. His detachment from them is at a peak. His noticing no longer enters into or settles down on any phenomena at all. At this moment, a consciousness arises that takes as its object the "signless, no-occurrence, no-formation": *nirvana*. Awareness of all physical and mental phenomena ceases entirely.

This moment of penetration of nirvana does not, in its first attainment, last even for a second. Immediately following this, the "fruition" moment occurs, when the meditator's mind reflects on the experience of nirvana just past. That experience is a cognitive shock of deepest psychological consequence. Because it is of a realm beyond that of the common-sense reality from which our language is generated, nirvana is a "supramundane reality," describable only in terms of what it is not. Nirvana has no phenomenology, no experiential characteristics. It is the unconditioned state.

Nirvana: Subsequent Changes

The word "nirvana" derives from the negative prefix "nir" and the root "vana," to burn, a metaphorical expression for the extinction of motives for becoming. In nirvana, desire, attachment, and self-interest are burned out. Decisive behavior changes follow from this state of consciousness, and the full realization of nirvana actuates a permanent alteration of the meditator's consciousness per se. With the meditator's realization of nirvana, aspects of his ego and of his normal consciousness are abandoned, never to arise again.

The path of insight differs significantly from the path

of concentration on this point: Nirvana destroys "defiling" aspects of mental states—hatred, greed, delusion, etc.—whereas jhana merely suppresses them. The fruit of nirvana for the meditator is effortless moral purity; in fact, purity becomes his only possible behavior. Jhana smothers the meditator's defilements, but their seeds remain latent in his personality as potentialities. On his emergence from the jhanic state, impure acts again become possible as appropriate trigger situations arise. To attain effortless purity, the meditator's egoism must "die," that is, all of his desires originating from self-interest must cease to control his behavior.

After insight has culminated in the nirvanic state, the meditator's mind remains free of certain motivations and psychological states, which no longer arise. On full maturation of insight, his purity is perfected. By then, he will have utterly given up the potential for impure acts. What was in the early stages effortful for the meditator becomes a self-maintaining state in which attitudes of purity are effortless, choiceless by-products of the state itself.

The number of times the meditator enters the nirvanic state determines his level of mastery, that is, his ability to attain nirvana whenever, wherever, as soon as, and for as long as he wants. But his level of mastery is not the same as nirvana-caused personality changes. He can enter nirvana with a given degree of insight countless times without any subsequent change of his being. The deeper he develops insight prior to entering nirvana, the greater the subsequent changes will be. The nature of nirvana itself is identical at each level of attainment. Since nirvana is the complete extinction of consciousness, it is always the same, though beyond experience. But there are differences between levels of nirvana-caused change. The differences are reckoned in terms of the meditator's consequent loss of ego and alteration in his normal consciousness after he has emerged from nirvana. Entering the nirvanic state is his "awakening"; these subsequent changes are his "deliverance."

The first level of deliverance is that of *Sotapanna*, "stream enterer," the "stream" entered being that leading to the total loss of his selfish ego, the cessation of all his strivings to become. The meditator becomes a stream enterer at the moment of reflection after his first penetration of nirvana. He remains a stream enterer until his insight deepens to the degree necessary to break through to the next level of attainment. This final liberation, it is said, is sure to occur "within seven more lifetimes." The stream enterer loses the following personality traits: his greed for sensory objects; any resentments strong enough to make him agitated; greed for his own gain, possessions, or praise; his inability to share with others; his failure to perceive the relative and illusory nature of whatever may seem pleasurable or beautiful; his mistaking for permanent what is impermanent (anicca); his seeing a self in what is devoid of self (anatta); his adherence to mere rites, compulsive ritualism, and any belief that this or that is "the truth"; and his doubts in the utility of the path of insight meditation. The stream enterer by nature can also no longer engage in lying, stealing, sexual misconduct, physically harming others, or earning his livelihood at the expense of others.

When the meditator's insight deepens so that the realizations of dukkha, anatta, or anicca more fully pervade his awareness, his insight intensifies a quantum level deeper. At this deeper level both his greed for sense desires and his ill will weaken further. In addition to what he abandoned with stream entry, the meditator lets go of gross desires for sense objects and strong resentment. He is now a *sakadgami*, "once returner," who will be fully liberated in this lifetime "or the next." The intensity of his feelings of attraction and aversion diminishes: He can no longer be strongly impelled toward or put off by anything. The pull of sex, for example, lessens; he can still have intercourse for procreation, but he will have no compulsive sexual needs. Impartiality typifies his reactions toward any and all stimuli.

At the next phase in the deepening of his insight, he abandons altogether both greed for sense desires and ill will. What was diminished when he reached the level of once returner is now wholly extinguished. The meditator is an *anagami*, "nonreturner," and he will be totally liberated from the wheel of becoming in his present lifetime. In addition to what he previously abandoned, his last remaining residual propensities toward greed or resentment drop away. All aversion to worldly states, such as loss, disgrace, pain, or blame, ceases. Maliciousness in motivation, volition, or speech becomes impossible for the nonreturner. He can no longer even have a thought of ill will toward anyone, and the category of "enemy" vanishes from his thinking, along with that of "dislike." Similarly, even his subtlest desire for sense objects disappears. Sexual activity, for example, is unlikely for the nonreturner because his feelings of lust are gone, as are his desires for sensual pleasures. Equanimity prevails toward all external objects; their valence to the nonreturner is absolutely neutral.

When the meditator's insight fully matures, he overcomes all remaining fetters to liberation. He is now an *arahant*, an "awakened being" or saint; the word arahant means "one who is worthy" of veneration. The arahant is free from his former socially conditioned identity; he sees consensual concepts of reality as illusions. He is absolutely free from suffering and from acting in a way that would further his karma. Having no feelings of "self," his acts are purely functional, either for maintenance of his body or for the good of others. The arahant does everything with physical grace. Nothing in his past can cause thoughts of greed, hatred, and the like to come to mind. His past deeds are erased as determinants of behavior, and he is free of his past conditioned habits. He lives fully in the moment; all his actions bespeak spontaneity. The last vestiges of egoism the meditator relinquishes in this final stage include: his desire to seek worldly gain, fame, pleasure, or praise; his desire for even the bliss of the material or formless jhanas; mental stiffness or agitation; covetousness of anything whatsoever. For the arahant, the least tendency toward an unvirtuous thought or deed is literally inconceivable.

With the full extinction of "unwholesome" roots—lust, aggression, and pride—as motives in the meditator's behavior, loving-kindness, altruistic joy, compassion, and equanimity emerge as bases for his actions. Behavior stemming from unwholesome motives is seen as "unskilled"; the arahant's acts are in this sense "skilled." His motives are totally pure. Dreaming, too, changes for the arahant; he has no dreams due to bodily states (e.g., dreams of being chased, being hot or cold) or because of his impressions of daily happenings, but he may have premonitory dreams that foreshadow future events. Though the arahant can experience bodily pain, he bears it with equanimity. A prominent trait of the arahant is unselfishness, likened in the Pali Canon to motherly love:

Even as a mother watches over her only begotten child, so let his heart and mind be filled with boundless love for all creatures, great and small, let him practice benevolence towards the whole world, above, below, across, without exception, and let him set himself utterly free from ill-will and enmity.

One who has "awakened" in this way is capable of a dual perception: "Knowing how everything actually is, and how everything appears." For the arahant, normal reality is perceived simultaneously with the validity of the "noble truths" of impermanence, suffering and non-selfhood. Both these perceptual levels are evident at every moment. For example, even worldly pleasures are a form of suffering. Wei Wu Wei (1968: p. 61) says of the meaning of suffering at the arahant's level of consciousness:

> When the Buddha found that he was Awake . . . it may be assumed that he observed that what hitherto he had regarded as happiness, as compared to suffering, was such no longer. His only standard henceforward was *ananda* or what we try to think of as bliss. Suffering he saw as the negative form of happiness, happiness as the positive form of suffering, respectively the negative and positive aspects of experience. But relative to the noumenal state which now alone he knew, both could be described . . . as *dukkha* (suffering.) *Dukkha* was the counterpart of *sukha* which implied "ease and well-being," . . . to the Buddha nothing phenomenal could appear to be *sukha* although in phenomenality it might so appear in contrast to *dukkha*.

The way the arahant might understand the truth of nonself is more straightforward. As D. T. Suzuki (1958:

p. 293) puts it, the arahant finds "by immediate knowledge that when one's heart was cleansed of the defilements of the ordinary ego-centered impulses and desires,
nothing was left there to claim itself as ego-residuum."
More simply, after the meditator has let go of his selfish
ego to become an arahant, he finds he has no "self" left.

For the arahant, perception in insight meditation is
perfected: He witnesses the most minute segments of his
mind's working, the chain of mind moments. According
to this tradition, the Buddha witnessed 17×10^{21} mind
moments in "the wink of an eye," each one distinct and
different from the one preceding and the one following
it. Like him, the arahant sees that the smallest pieces of
the mosaic of consciousness are changing at every moment. Nothing in the universe of his mind is constant.
Since his external reality flows from his internal universe, nowhere can he find any stability or permanence.

Total Cessation

There is a state similar to nirvana (little known in the
West) called *nirodh* (cessation). In nirvana, awareness has
as its object the cessation of consciousness; in nirodh,
awareness ceases altogether. This absolute cessation of
consciousness is extremely difficult to attain. Nirodh is
accessible only to a nonreturner or an arahant, and only
if he has also mastered all eight jhanas. Neither a stream
enterer nor a once returner has given up enough ego-
bound attachments to muster the superconcentration
required for nirodh. In gaining access to this state of total
nonoccurrence, even the slightest sense desire is an ob-
stacle.

On the path to nirodh, the meditator practices insight,

using as a base each jhana in succession up to the eighth, "neither perception nor nonperception." With the cessation of this last state of ultrasubtle consciousness, he enters nirodh. The cessation of nirodh is said to be "differently real," for all the data of our experience of reality, even the most subtle states, are absent.

Although nirodh can last for up to seven days of the human time rhythm, there is no time sequence in the state itself: The moment immediately preceding and that immediately following it seem in succession. The limit of seven days given for nirodh may be due to its unique physiology. The meditator's heartbeat and normal metabolism, it is said, cease along with consciousness (or, more likely, continue below the threshold of perception). Metabolic processes continue at a residual level, and the meditator's body does not decay like a corpse. The meditator must set a predetermined length of time for his stay in this state before he enters. On emerging from it, he goes through the jhanas in reverse order to normal consciousness. At the eighth jhana, awareness resumes; at the third, normal bodily function; at the first, thoughts and sense perception.

At their highest extremes, the path of concentration through the jhanas and the path of insight to nirvana tend to meet. Even so, there remain extremely subtle but crucial differences between these rarefied states of consciousness. In the seventh jhana, "no-thing-ness," awareness is of objectless consciousness. In the eighth jhana, even no-thing-ness is not present; yet it remains as a latent function, and so no-thing-ness cannot be said *not* to exist: this is the supersubtle realm of "neither perception nor nonperception." In nirvana, consciousness is on the brink of extinction with the awareness of no consciousness at all. The cessation of awareness culminates in nirodh, in which there is no awareness whatsoever. Attaining even the highest jhanas does not lastingly alter the meditator's personality, while nirvana does so irrevocably.

These different paths mark two extremes in exploring and controlling the mind. A meditator who could marshal enough one-pointedness to attain the formless jhanas might easily enter the nirvanic state should he choose to turn his powerful concentration to watching his own mind. Conversely, a meditator who had entered the nirvanic state might well be so indifferent to hindrances and distractions that, should he choose to focus on a single object of awareness, he would readily enter and proceed through the jhanic levels. Those who traverse these distinctly different paths to their summits, then, may no longer belong solely to one but to both. With full mastery of either samadhi or insight, the other is readily attainable. At their end, the distinction between meditation avenues melts.

PART TWO

MEDITATION PATHS:
A SURVEY

EXPERIENCE IS the forerunner of all spiritual teachings, but the same experience can be expressed differently. In any given tradition, the map of meditative states set down is to some degree arbitrary. The map is not the terrain, and the territory traversed in meditation is nebulous to begin with. It is little wonder that maps of meditative states seem so different from one another. Lao Tzu recognizes this dilemma in the Tao Te Ching:

> The way that can be told
> Is not the constant way;
> The name that can be named
> Is not the constant name.

The Tibetans recognize two levels of religion: "the expedient teaching" and "the final teaching." The expedient teachings are the multitude of world religions, each shaped by and for the people who adhere to it. Part of the differences between meditation maps stem from this level. The survey of meditation maps in this chapter is aimed at the level of final teaching, in which doctrinal differences fall away. Here the unity of practice comes into focus. Religions may differ by virtue of accident of time and place, but the experiences that are precursors to beliefs are often the same. Some degree of unity in final teaching is inevitable: All human beings are alike in nervous system, and it is at this level that the laws governing final teaching operate.

The Visuddhimagga map undercuts seeming distinctions between spiritual paths in meditation techniques and states. These distinctions, in fact, stem from different ideologies. The Visuddhimagga road maps give us a typology for sorting out techniques in terms of their mechanics, cutting through the conceptual overlay of religions. This survey is meant to be seminal, not exhaustive. In most cases, I discuss only one illustrative technique of the many disciplines belonging to a given spiritual path. This comparison is one of parts, of specific practices and states, rather than a taxonomy of spiritual paths.

I based most of the summaries that follow on published sources rather than on my personal investigation. They may, therefore, seem incomplete or imprecise to a person on any of these paths. Each path is a living tradition that presents itself differently to each person according to his needs and circumstances.

The summaries are didactic, not definitive. My intent is to give those not involved in them an idea of what they are like. I discuss each path in enough detail to show its unique flavor, while demonstrating its points of similarity with other paths.

4. HINDU BHAKTI

Sri Ramakrishna, a Bengali saint at the turn of the century, once went to a theater performance of the life of Sri Chaitanya, the seventeenth-century Bhakti saint known for his songs and dances of love for Lord Krishna. At several points during the play, on seeing portrayals of Chaitanya's devotion to Krishna, Ramakrishna entered samadhi, a deep meditative absorption.

Ramakrishna's samadhi marks him as a Bhakta par excellence. Bhakti, or devotion to a divine being, is the most popular form of worship in contemporary world religions. A Christian singing "Amazing Grace," a Hassidic Jew dancing and singing at the Wailing Wall, a Sufi reciting "El Allah Hu," a Hindu chanting "Hare Krishna," and a Japanese Buddhist repeating "Na-mu-a-mi-da-bu-tsu, Na-mu-a-mi-da-bu-tsu" are all engaged in more or less the same devotional process, though directed toward different divine beings.

Bhakti is the strongest school of religious practice in Hinduism; its roots are ancient. In the classic *Srimad Bhagavatam,* remembering or constant chanting of Krishna's name is recommended over all other practices as the best path for this age. The *Kalisantaram Upanishad* has Brahma extol to the bard Narada as the highest or *maha*-mantra, "Hare Rama, Hare Krishna"—Hare, Rama, and Krishna all being manifestations of Vishnu. The essence of Bhakti is making the object of devotion one's central thought. The devotee may choose any deity or divine being as his devotional object, or *ishta*. The thrust of his practice is to keep the thought of the ishta foremost in his mind at all times. Besides *kirtan* (chanting or singing), there are three levels of *japa*, repetition of the name: spoken, silent verbalization, and mental. Some regard each succeeding form of japa as "ten times" more efficacious than the preceding one (Poddar, 1965).

Poddar suggests that the neophyte practice a minimum of six hours of japa per day. From the beginning, the devotee also strives to maintain japa in the midst of life's activities. The *mala*, or rosary, is a common technical aid to japa; with the telling of each bead, the devotee recites the name once. Other aids include gearing recitation to each breath or to every beat of the pulse. No matter what the mnemonic device, the principle is the same: The devotee returns his attention to the ishta at once whenever his mind ceases to be engaged elsewhere. The goal of this stage of practice is to make the habit of repetition stronger than all the devotee's other mental habits. Gradually, his mind will be occupied solely with the thought of the deity or centered on it as other thoughts come and go on the periphery of awareness. In this way, the devotee becomes one-pointed on his ishta.

Some advice to the devotee repeats the Visuddhimagga. Because the mental habit of constant worship through remembering is at first vulnerable to other pulls for attention, the devotee is urged to keep to *satsang*, the company of persons on the same path. Staying with satsang counters the pull of worldly attachments, as does *darshan*, the visiting of saints. The devotee is further urged to avoid talk of "women, wealth, unbelievers, and enemies." The devotee's success depends on virtue: Purity, says Vivekananda (1964), "is absolutely the basic work, the bedrock upon which the whole Bhakti-building rests." In giving advice to her own disciples, Ananda Mayee Ma, a contemporary Indian woman saint, echoes the Visuddhimagga's for Buddhist monks (1972: pp. 126–29):

Indolence and lust—these two are the greatest obstacles on the path . . . Choose carefully and abide
strictly by such occupations as awaken godly
thoughts and feelings . . . Engage in them even
when there is no desire so to do, as one takes medicine . . . Food, sleep, toilet, clothes, etc., should be
given only as much attention as is needed for the
maintenance of health . . . Anger, greed and the
like must be altogether abandoned. Neither should
you be swayed by praise or prestige.

The guru's help ranks in importance with purity for
the devotee's progress. Ananda Mayee Ma (1972) com-
pares the role of the guru to that of experts in any spe-
cialized field to whom one must turn in order to become
proficient. But the function of the guru transcends that of
the worldly expert. In addition to directing the disciple,
the guru is also the intermediary for divine grace needed
for the disciple's efforts to bear fruit. No matter how dili-
gent the devotee, without the guru's blessings his efforts
are useless.

Ramana Maharshi (1962) says of "Guru-kripa," surrender to a master whose grace descends on the devotee. "If
one's surrender is complete, all sense of self is lost."
When the devotee surrenders to the pure being of the
guru, his mind becomes purified. The purified mind easily stills, allowing the devotee to turn inward in meditation and find the self. This is the guru's "grace," which is
in fact immanent in the devotee. There is, says Ramana
Maharshi, no difference between God, guru, and self:
The external guru helps the devotee find the internal self
in meditation. The outer guide leads the devotee back
within himself.

As in all paths, virtue—in the beginning an act of

will—becomes a by-product of the practice itself. As the devotee's mind focuses on his devotional object, it withdraws from worldly objects. By love of God, says Vivekananda, love of the pleasures of the senses and of the intellect is all made dim. As his consciousness becomes more thoroughly imbued with the thought of his ishta, the devotee finds worldly delights repugnant. By this point, observes Poddar (1965), "compared to the joy of repeating the 'Rama nama' (i.e., mantra) all other enjoyments of the world are insipid."

Bhakti begins in duality, with the devotee separate from his ishta, as from any love object. The *Bhakti Sutras*, in fact, have a typology of Divine Love that includes loving the ishta as one's friend, as one's spouse, and as one's child. Prabhavananda and Isherwood (1969) suggest that "all human relationships may be sublimated through the practice of Bhakti yoga." Though this love may begin with the forms of, and energies invested in, interpersonal love, it ends in union with the state of love evoked by the love object. Here, says Vivekananda, "Love, the Lover, and the Beloved are One." With this union, Bhakti merges into the path of jhana. The fruit of japa is constant remembrance at every waking moment of the beloved. This yields a "love intoxication"; its signs are ecstasy and absorption. The feelings of bliss, rapture, and joy of this intoxication characterize access concentration. The love-intoxicated devotee's behavior, however, is sometimes as erratic as a madman's. The *Srimad Bhagavata* (XI, ii) describes this stage:

> . . . the devotee loses all sense of decorum and moves about in the world unattached . . . His heart melts through love as he habitually chants the Name of his beloved lord, and like one possessed, he now

bursts into peals of laughter, now weeps, now cries, now sings aloud and now begins to dance.

The enraptured devotee is on the threshold of samadhi, or jhana. His ecstasy indicates the access level; he verges on the first jhana. Should he concentrate with enough intensity on his ishta, he can enter samadhi. Once samadhi is reached, according to Swami Muktananda (1971), there is no further need for chanting or japa: They are a prelude to the deep meditation of samadhi. An accomplished bhakta can attain samadhi on the least stimulus, suggesting his devotion, as did Sri Ramakrishna.

The initial power of Bhakti is the element of interpersonal love felt by the devotee toward his deity. As he progresses on this path, that love changes from an interpersonal to a transcendental or transpersonal love. The devotee no longer depends on the object of devotion to bestow bliss. Rather, he finds that the transcendental states of which the bliss is one aspect exist within himself. He need no longer cling to the external form of his devotional object; the states once evoked by his beloved's form have come to be fixtures of his own consciousness. Sankaracharya, the founder of Advait Hinduism, noted that Bhakti ends in a quest for the self: What begins as an external evocation of love becomes in the end an internal absorption in which the devotee in samadhi delights uninterruptedly in "pure self."

The devotee brings his mind to one-pointedness through constant remembrance of the ishta and so finally reaches samadhi at the level of first jhana. But if he is to go beyond this level, he must transcend his own devotional object. Any thought of name and form, even that of a deity, binds the devotee to the first jhana. Sri Ra-

makrishna, for example, for many years an ardent devotee of the Divine Mother, had experienced many visions
and states of bliss as Her devotee. Later, he took initiation from a naked ascetic (Swami Saradananda, 1963:
p. 255):

> After initiating me . . . the Naked One asked me to
> make my mind free of function in all respects, and
> merge in the meditation of the Self. But, when I sat
> for meditation, I could by no means make my mind
> go beyond the bounds of name and form and cease
> functioning. The mind withdrew itself from all
> other things, but as soon as it did so, the intimately
> familiar form of the universal Mother appeared . . .
> But, at last, collecting all the strength of my will, I
> cut Mother's form to pieces with the sword of dis-
> crimination . . . There remained no function in the
> mind, which transcended quickly the realm of
> names and forms, making me merge in samadhi.

The Visuddhimagga says that on initial entry to a new
plane of meditative consciousness the meditator must cut
his ties to the preceding plane. Each plane has its special
points of appeal, some exceedingly sublime. The
prerequisite for gaining the next higher level is to become
detached from the lower plane, as Ramakrishna did, lest
awareness be pulled back to it. For the devotee, this
means that his ishta's form must finally be abandoned in
favor of becoming himself, in samadhi, that manifesta-
tion of pure being for which the ishta is himself wor-
shiped.

Beyond the attainment of samadhi, there is a state in
which a samadhilike awareness diffuses throughout all
the devotee's activities. Japa, if developed to this point,

repeats as if of itself virtually every moment, day and night. This state is *sahaj samadhi* and marks the end point in the devotee's spiritual evolution. In sahaj samadhi, there is no distinction between the devotee, the world, and the ishta; his perception of self and the world shifts radically. As Vivekananda (1964: p. 90) puts it, "When a person loves the Lord, the whole universe becomes dear to him . . . his whole nature is purified and completely changed." Renunciation becomes effortless, all attachments save to the beloved ishta having fallen away.

From this intense and all-absorbing love comes faith and self-surrender, the conviction that nothing that happens is against one: "Not my, but Thy will be done." This selflessness is evident in the words of Ananda Mayee Ma, speaking of herself (1972: p. 37): "Truly this body belongs to all; for this reason it behaves and speaks, as far as possible, so as to fulfill the needs of the people with whom it deals at any particular time." One at this ultimate point on the Bhakti path perceives the sacred within the secular; everything is sacred because it bespeaks the beloved. The devotee need no longer observe any special forms or symbols for worship. He worships in his heart, the world having become his altar. Kabir (1970: pp. 48–49) eloquently sums up his own experience of this state:

> O Sadhu! the simple union is the best,
> Since the day when I met with my Lord, there has been no end to the sport of our love.
> I shut not my eyes, I close not my ears, I do not mortify my body;
> I see with eyes open and smile, and behold His beauty everywhere;
> I utter His Name, and whatever I see, it reminds me of Him; whatever I do, it becomes His worship.

The rising and setting are one to me; all contradictions are solved.

Wherever I go, I move round Him,

All I achieve is His service:

When I lie down, I lie prostrate at His feet.

He is the only adorable one to me: I have none
other.

My tongue has left off impure words, it sings His
glory day and night:

Whether I rise or sit down, I can never forget Him;
for the rhythm of His music beats in my ears.

Kabir says, I am immersed in the one great bliss
which transcends all pleasure and pain.

5. JEWISH KABBALAH

"In every religion," writes the contemporary Kabbalist
Z'ev ben Shimon Halevi (1976), "there are always two
aspects, the seen and the hidden." The seen manifests as
rituals, scriptures, services; the hidden bears the light
that should illumine these forms. In Judaism, the hidden
teachings are called Kabbalah. These teachings, it is said,
originated with the angels, who were instructed by God.
Kabbalists identify the great figures of Biblical times—
Abraham, David, the Prophets—as well as the Essenes
and other mystical groups of Jewish history, as bearers of
this tradition. Halevi says Joshua ben Miriam, otherwise
known as Jesus, was a transmitter of Kabbalah. This hidden Jewish tradition first surfaced in Europe in the Middle Ages, and many lineages of its transmission continue
to the present day.

The cosmology of Kabbalah posits a multileveled reality, each level a complete world in itself. These planes are arranged hierarchically, the upper part of each corresponding to the lower aspect of the one above. The highest sphere is that of Metatron, the chief archangel, who teaches human beings. Each level embodies a state of consciousness, and most people exist at the lowest levels—mineral, vegetable, animal. In the Kabbalist view, normal man is incomplete, restricted as he is to these lower planes. He lives a mechanical life, bound by the rhythms of his body and by habitual reactions and perceptions; he blindly seeks pleasure and avoids pain. While he may have brief glimpses of higher possibilities, he has no desire to raise his level of awareness. Kabbalah seeks to awaken the student to his own limitations and to train him to enter a state of consciousness in which he becomes in tune with a higher awareness, no longer a slave of his body and conditioning. To become free, the aspirant must first become disillusioned with the mechanical games of life. He then builds a foundation for entry into a higher consciousness, the Paradise within. This, says Halevi, is the allegorical meaning of the bondage in Egypt: the slavery of the limited ego, the seeker's purification in the desert, and his entry into the land of milk and honey.

To achieve his task, the Kabbalist must observe the working of the *Yesod*, his ordinary mind or ego, so as to see through his own foibles and self-delusions and bring into awareness the unconscious forces that shape his thoughts and actions. To do this, he seeks to reach the level of awareness called *Tiferet*, a state of clarity that is witness or "watcher" of the Yesod. From this state of heightened self-awareness emanates what is sometimes seen as a guardian angel that guides one through difficult situations with ease and skill. Tiferet is beyond the ordinary mind dealing with everyday matters; here ego is transcended. It is the realm of the spirit, the bridge between man and the divine, the gate of Paradise. It is the soul. Thus, in a state of Yesod, the ego rules; when Tiferet is dominant, a higher state occurs in which one looks down on oneself. This state of awakened consciousness is typically glimpsed only briefly in the ordinary man's life. The Kabbalist seeks to gain permanent entry to this state and ascend to even higher levels still.

The specifics of the Kabbalist's training—his foundation for higher states—vary from school to school, though the basics are fairly constant. When the aspirant contacts a *Maggid*, or teacher, his training begins in earnest. The Maggid directs him in candid self-observation, using the stuff of the student's life as material for teaching. There are many systems that aid the seeker in knowing himself, such as an intricate numerology that transmutes Hebrew letters and words into a number code with mystical interpretations. One of the best-known Kabbalist systems is the Tree of Life, a map of the hierarchies and attributes of the many planes that interplay in the world and within man. The tree serves as a template through which the aspirant observes his own nature and a key to unlock the hidden dimensions guiding his life. But a mere intellectual understanding of the tree may be Yesodic, in the service of the ego. No matter how elegantly the seeker grasps the intricacies of the tree, his studies will be for naught if he neglects his spiritual development. The prerequisite is training of his will, his capacity for unwavering attention. For this the Kabbalist turns to meditation. Writes Halevi (1976: p. 126):

Preparation means to be able to receive and impart . . . the degree of reception determines the quality of Knowledge given. The exchange is precise, and is

paid for by the amount of conscious attention in a
complex situation. Where attention is, there is
power.

The instructions for meditation form part of the secret
teachings of Kabbalists and, apart from general rules, are
not made public. Each student learns from the mouth of
his Maggid. In general, meditation in Kabbalah is an
offshoot of the normal prayers of the devout Jew. Meditative concentration allows the Kabbalist to delve to the
depths of a particular subject—a word in a prayer or an
aspect of the tree—and also to arrest his thought so as to
remain one-pointed on the subject. This fine focus is *kavvanah*, cleaving of thought to a single subject. In one sort
of kavvanah, the meditator concentrates on each word of
regular prayer with his full attention, to the point at
which his mind transcends the simple meaning of the
words, and so uses them as a vehicle to a higher state.
Azriel of Gerona, a medieval Kabbalist, described the
process of kavvanah as when "thought expands and as-
cends to its origin, so that when it reaches it, it ends and
cannot ascend any further." As a result of this state, the
words of the prayer become transmuted, full of a divine
influx from this nothingness of thought.

According to Kabbalist lore, the entry into the inner
Paradise by one who has not properly prepared a foundation through self-purification can be dangerous. The Tal-
mud tells the story of four rabbis who entered Paradise:
one went mad, one died, and another lost faith; only one,
Rabbi Akiba, came back in peace. The influential writings of Abraham Abulafia, among the most detailed elab-
oration of Kabbalist meditation, were designed to teach a
safe approach to the inner Paradise. Abulafia's meditation
combines various letters of the Hebrew alphabet in a

meditation on the holy names of God. This method is distinct from prayer; the aspirant devoted himself to it in seclusion rather than in synagogue, at given hours and under guidance of his Maggid. Halevi describes the path traveled by one who practices such a meditation. As he repeats the name, he directs his attention upward from Yesod, the limited ordinary mind, into Tiferet, an awareness beyond ego. That is, he directs his thought away from all forms of this world, focusing on the name. If his efforts meet with God's grace, the self will suddenly rise up beyond Tiferet to an ecstatic state called *Daat*, or knowledge. Here his sense of separation from God dissolves, if only for a moment. He is filled with a great joy, and seized by a sweet rapture. When he emerges from this state, he will again become aware of the inner repetition of the name, which he had transcended for that instant in a state the Theravadans might call jhana.

The end of the Kabbalist's path is *devekut*, in which the seeker's soul cleaves to God. When the Kabbalist stabilizes his consciousness at this level, he is no longer an ordinary man but a supernatural man, a *Zaddik*, or saint, who has escaped the chains of his personal ego. The qualities of one who has attained this station include equanimity, indifference to praise or blame, a sense of being alone with God, and prophecy. The ego's will is submerged in the divine will so that one's acts serve God rather than a limited self. He need no longer study Torah, for he has *become* Torah. One classical commentator defines devekut as a state of mind in which (Scholem, 1974: p. 175):

You constantly remember God and his love, nor do you remove your thought from Him . . . to the point when such a person speaks with someone else, his heart is not with them at all but is still before God. And indeed it may be true of those who attain this rank, that their soul is granted immortal life even in this lifetime, for they are themselves a dwelling place for the Holy Spirit.

6. CHRISTIAN HESYCHASM

The first Christian monks were hermits who lived during the fourth century A.D. in the most remote parts of the barren Egyptian desert. A record from that time (Waddell, 1957: p. 57) has it that "once a certain brother brought a bunch of grapes to the holy Macarius," one of the hermits. But the hermit

> who for love's sake thought not on his own things but on the things of others, carried it to another brother, who seemed more feeble. And the sick man gave thanks to God for the kindness of his brother, but he too thinking more of his neighbor than himself, brought it to another, and he again to another, and so that same bunch of grapes was carried round all the cells scattered as they were far over the desert, and no one knowing who first had sent it, it was brought at last to the first giver.

The Desert Fathers, like present-day Indian yogis in the high Himalayas, sought out the isolation of the harshest desert to commune with God free of worldly distractions. The meditation practices and rules for living of these earliest Christian monks bear strong similarity to those of their Hindu and Buddhist renunciate brethren several kingdoms to the east. While Jesus and his teachings were their inspiration, the meditative techniques they adopted for finding their God suggest either a borrowing from the East or a spontaneous rediscovery. The ways of the Desert Fathers influence Christian monasticism to this day; their selfless love remains a guiding example.

Constant remembrance of God—much as the Bhakti and the Kabbalist aim for—has been a mainstay of Christian worship from the beginning, though the present-day use of rosary beads is a dim remainder of more wholehearted remembrance. Thomas Merton (1960) observes that what is today practiced as "prayer" in Christian churches is but one—albeit the surviving one—of a range of more intensive contemplative practices. The Desert Fathers meditated with verbal or silent repetition of a single phrase from the Scriptures, a Christian equivalent of mantra. The most popular was the prayer of the Publican: "Lord Jesus Christ, Son of God, have mercy on me a sinner." In its short form, *Kyrie eleison*, it was repeated silently throughout the day "until it became as spontaneous and instinctive as breathing."

The Desert Fathers emphasized purity, and their ascetic acts are fabled; St. Simeon the Stylite, who lived thirty years atop a pillar, was one of the best known. As in the Visuddhimagga, purification was used to aid concentration; in the words of one of the fathers, "the soul, unless it be cleansed of alien thoughts, cannot pray to God in contemplation." A corollary maxim is that life in the world matters only insofar as it reflects an inner life of contemplative practice. The spirit of this tradition,

preserved in modern monastic orders such as the Benedictine Trappists, is summed up by St. Abba Dorotheus,
an early Desert Father, in giving directions on spiritual
training (Kadloubovsky and Palmer, 1969: p. 161):

> Over whatever you have to do, even if it be very
> urgent and demands great care, I would not have
> you argue or be agitated. For rest assured, every-
> thing you do, be it great or small, is but one-eighth
> of the problem, whereas to keep one's state undis-
> turbed even if thereby one should fail to accomplish
> the task, is the other seven-eighths. So if you are
> busy at some task and wish to do it perfectly, try to
> accomplish it—which, as I said would be one-eighth
> of the problem, and at the same time to preserve
> your state unharmed—which constitutes seven-
> eighths. If, however, in order to accomplish your
> task you would inevitably be carried away and harm
> yourself or another by arguing with him, you should
> not lose seven for the sake of preserving one-eighth.

One major tradition stemming from the practices of
the Desert Fathers, though virtually lost in Western
Christendom, has changed little in Eastern Orthodoxy
since the first millenium of Christianity. This is the practice of the Prayer of Jesus. Its repetition fulfills Paul's in-
junction to "pray always." The early fathers called it "the
art of arts and the science of sciences," which leads the
seeker toward the highest human perfection. This tradition is preserved in the collection of early Christian writings known as the *Philokalia* (Kadloubovsky and Palmer,
1971). Its translation from Greek to Russian at the turn
of the century came on the crest of a wave of revival of
the practice throughout Russia (French, 1970).

The practice of the Prayer develops strength of concentration. As in Hindu Bhakti, the prerequisites for success with the Prayer are "genuine humility, sincerity, endurance, purity." Hesychius of Jerusalem, a fifth-century teacher of the uses of the Jesus Prayer (known now in the West as Hesychasm), describes it as a spiritual art that releases one completely from passionate thoughts, words, and evil deeds, and gives a "sure knowledge of God the Incomprehensible." Practice of the Prayer brings purity of heart, which is the "same as guarding the mind, kept perfectly free of all fantasies" and all thoughts. The way to this purity is unceasingly calling upon Christ, with perfect attention, resisting all other thoughts. Hesychius describes thoughts as "enemies who are bodiless and invisible, malicious and clever at harming us, skillful, nimble and practised in warfare," who enter in through the five senses. A mind caught in the senses or in thought is distant from Jesus. To overcome sense consciousness and attain a silent mind is to be with Him.

Among the "Directions to Hesychasts" is the instruction to find a teacher who bears the spirit within him. Once found, the seeker devotes himself to his master, obeying all his commands. Other directions include seclusion in a quiet, dimly lit cell, eating only as much as one needs to keep alive, silence, full performance of church ritual, fasting, vigils, and most important, practice of the Prayer.

The *Philokalia* quotes St. Nilus: "He who wishes to see what his mind really is must free himself of all thoughts; then he will see it like a sapphire or the hue of heaven." His instructions for stilling the mind specify sitting on a low stool in the solitude of one's cell on first awakening and for an hour (or more, if one is able), "collect your mind from its customary circling and wandering outside, and quietly lead it into the heart by way of breathing, keeping this prayer: 'Lord Jesus Christ, Son of God, have mercy on me!' connected with the breath." When with practice it becomes possible to so pray with perfect one-pointedness, "then, abandoning the many and the varied, we shall unite with the One, the Single and the Unifying, directly in a union which transcends reason"— presumably, in jhana.

Prayer is not to be limited to specific sessions but practiced without distraction in the midst of every activity. The Prayer so performed brings purity to worldly activity. The monk who has mastered this ability has the stature of Christ because he enjoys perfect purity of heart. The goal of the Desert Fathers' efforts was what Merton calls a "nowhereness and no-mindness"—a condition known by the name *quies*, literally "rest"—the monk having lost all preoccupation with his limited self. Combined with ascetic life in the desert, these prayer practices, in the words of Merton, "enabled the old superficial self to be purged away and permitted the gradual emergence of the true, secret self in which the Believer and Christ were 'one spirit'." St. Isaac comments that one who has attained a state of effortless, constant prayer (Kadloubovsky and Palmer, 1971: p. 213):

> . . . has reached the summit of all virtues, and has become the abode of the Holy Spirit . . . when the Holy Spirit comes to live in a man, he never ceases to pray, for then the Holy Spirit constantly prays in him . . . In eating or drinking, sleeping or doing something, even in deep sleep his heart sends forth without effort the incense and sighs of prayer.

The themes of acts of purification, deep meditation, and finally their fruition in spontaneous purity and constant remembrance of God are not unique to Eastern Orthodoxy's Hesychasts. These central threads are widespread in Catholic contemplative traditions. St. Augustine, for one, advocated these same basic practices. Furthermore, the similarity of entry into jhana and the union with the One of the Christian mystic is clear in St. Augustine's *Confessions*. Augustine advocated a long process of self-denial, self-conquest, and the practice of virtue as preparation for "the ascent to the contemplation of God." Only such ascetic self-discipline can bring about the readjustment of character prerequisite for entry into the higher stages of a spiritual life. Augustine is insistent that not until the monk has so become "cleansed and healed" can he begin the proper practice of what he calls "contemplation." Contemplation itself entails "recollection" and "introversion." Recollection is concentrating the mind, banishing all images, thoughts, and sense perceptions. Having emptied the mind of all distractions, introversion can begin. Introversion concentrates the mind on its own deepest part in what is seen as the final step before the soul finds God: "The mind abstracts itself from all the bodily senses, as interrupting and confounding it with their din, in order to see itself in itself." So seeing, the soul arrives at God "in and above itself." Augustine describes the physical side of the state induced by this experience in terms like the Visuddhimagga's for jhana (Butler, 1966: p. 50):

> When the attention of the mind is wholly turned away and withdrawn from the bodily senses, it is called an ecstasy. Then whatever bodies may be

present are not seen with the open eyes, nor any voices heard at all. It is a state midway between sleep and death: The soul is rapt in such wise as to be withdrawn from the bodily senses more than in sleep, but less than in death.

St. Benedict's still definitive *Rule for Monasteries* depicts this progression in terms of degrees of "humility" or purity. At the twelfth and highest degree, the monk not only seems by all appearances to be humble but also has a genuine internal humility. His humility stems from a constant thought very much like the Prayer of the Publican: "Lord I am a sinner and not worthy to lift up my eyes to heaven." At this point, formerly effortful self-discipline becomes effortless (Doyle, 1948: p. 28–29):

Having climbed all these steps of humility, therefore, the monk will presently come to that perfect love of God which casts out fear. And all those precepts which formerly he had not observed without fear, he will now begin to keep by reason of that love, without any effort, as though naturally and by habit. No longer will his motive be the fear of hell, but rather the love of Christ, good habit and delight in the virtues which the Lord will deign to show forth by the Holy Spirit in His servant now cleaned from vice and sin.

7. SUFISM

For the Sufi, the basic human weakness is being bound
by the lower self. The saints have overcome their lower
nature, and novices seek to escape it. Meditation is essential in the novice's efforts to purify his heart. "Meditation
for one hour," said an early Sufi master, "is better than
ritual worship for a whole year."

The main meditation among Sufis is *zikr*, which means
"remembrance." The zikr par excellence is *La ilāha illā
'llah*: "There is no god but God." Bishi al-Hafi, an early
Sufi of Baghdad, said, "The Sufi is he who keeps his
Heart pure." The Sufi aims for a purity that is total and
permanent. The way to this purity is constant remembrance of God. The Prophet Muhammed himself said,
"There is a polish for everything that taketh away rust;
and the polish of the Heart is the invocation of Allah."
Remembrance of God through repeating his name puri-
fies the seeker's mind and opens his heart to Him. A zikr,
for example, always accompanies Sufi dancing; it en-
hances the dance's effect to maintain the remembrance of
God throughout. "The dance opens a door in the soul to
divine influences," wrote Sultan Walad, Rumi's son.
"The dance is good when it arises from remembrance of
the Beloved."

Zikr is also a solitary meditation. At first, it is an oral
repetition, later a silent one; a fourteenth-century manu-
script says, "When the heart begins to recite, the tongue
should stop." The goal of zikr, as in all meditation systems, is to overcome the mind's natural state of care-
lessness and inattention. His mind mastered, the Sufi can
become one-pointed on God. The Sufi comment on normal consciousness is that humans are "asleep in a night-

mare of unfulfilled desires," that with the transcendence
mental discipline brings, these desires fall away.

The normal state of attention—scattered and random,
thoughtless and heedless—is the mode of the profane.
Remembrance, which anchors the Sufi's mind on God,
focuses his attention and allows him to turn away from
the pulls of the world. A ninth-century Egyptian Sufi
commented on the special efforts the seeker makes: "The
repentance of the masses is from sins, whereas repentance of the elect is from distraction." After intensive
practice of meditation or group chanting, the following
relaxation of efforts may bring a floodtide of old habits of
mind. The degree of such a relapse serves as a gauge of
spiritual progress. No virtue is acquired if the conditioned habits and reactions take control as soon as the
seeker's intensity lessens.

There is an interplay between effort and grace on the
Sufi path. An eleventh-century itinerary of the Sufi path
by al-Qushari lists the spiritual stations (*maqam*) due to
one's own efforts. These purificatory acts prepare the
Sufi for achieving states (*hal*) that are independent of his
own effort. These effortless states are the gift of God.
The first station is that of "conversion," in which the
Sufi resolves to abandon worldly life and devote himself
to spiritual seeking. Then come a number of efforts at
self-purification. These include outright struggle against
his own carnal nature, helped by withdrawal into solitude for ridding himself of evil habits. At this stage, the
Sufi may minimize his involvement in worldly activities
and renounce even wholesome pleasures ordinarily permitted him. He may become a voluntary pauper, accept-
ing his tribulations as tests of purity and practicing con-
tentment with whatever comes his way. This last station

merges into the first God-given state, satisfaction with things as they are ordained by God.

The central premise supporting these renunciatory acts permeates Sufi thought: Abu Said of Mineh framed it as follows (Rice, 1964: p. 34): "When occupied with self, you are separated from God. The way to God is but one step; the step out of yourself." Al-Ghazali, a twelfth-century legalist turned Sufi, commented on the essence of the way of the Sufi (Nicholson, 1929: p. 39):

> . . . the gift of the doctrine lies in overcoming the appetites of the flesh and getting rid of its evil dispositions and vile qualities, so that the heart may be cleared of all but God; and the means of clearing it is dhikr Allah, commemoration of God and the concentration of every thought upon Him.

Along his way to desirelessness, the Sufi undergoes states typical of progress in many other kinds of meditation. *Qurb* is a sense of God's constant nearness induced by concentration on Him. In *mahabba*, the Sufi loses himself in awareness of his beloved. Among the fruits of mahabba are visions and the "station of unity," where zikr (the remembrance), *zakir* (the one who remembers), and *mazkur* (the one remembered) become one. A Theravadan Buddhist might see these experiences as entry into first jhana. Sufis recognize mastery at the point when the zakir's attention fixes on the zikr without effort, driving out other thoughts from his mind. Sufis see this state, called *fana*, as a pure gift of grace in which the zakir is "lost in Truth." Fana means "passing away in God." It is attained, notes Arberry (1972), when "self as well as the world has been cast aside." The cessation of both internal and external awareness in one-pointed focus on the zikr marks the Sufi's absorption of fana as comparable to the Buddhist's jhana.

Practice in the Sufi way extends to every waking moment, as is evident in directions for one technique of a proto-Sufi order (Bennett, 1973: p. 34): "Be present at every breath. Do not let your attention wander for the duration of a single breath. Remember yourself always and in all situations." The extension of practice to all situations culminates in *baqa,* abiding in some degree of fana consciousness while in the midst of ordinary activity. The tenth-century Sufi al-Junaid of Baghdad gives a classic definition of fana as "dying-to-self," which carries over as baqa, "life-in-Him." In this transition, the Sufi does not cease to function as an individual; rather, his nature becomes perfected. The Sufi Idries Shah (1971) speaks of this change in terms of an "extra dimension of being" operating parallel to ordinary cognition and calls it "objective consciousness." Others speak of an inner transformation wherein the Sufi acquires "reflexes that conform to spiritual reality."

Sufis insist that their teaching must never be fixedly dogmatic but flexible enough to fit the needs of specific persons, times, and places. As one modern teacher, Sufi Abdul-Hamid, puts it (Shah, 1972: p. 60): "The Work is carried out by the teacher in accordance with his perception of the situation in which he finds himself. This means that there is no textbook, no system, no method, other than that which belongs to the school of the moment." There have been many guidebooks prepared for the Sufi seeker in different times and places. One such is Abu al-Najib's (1975) twelfth-century *A Sufi Rule for Novices,* a classical manual of the Sufi path. Though this

Sufi rule may bear little resemblance to contemporary practice, it allows us useful glimpses into the specifics of Sufi method and instructive comparisons to other spiritual paths.

Ibn al-Najib (1097–1168 A.D.) set down his rules for conduct for beginners in the Suhrwardi order to which he belonged; its purpose is comparable to that of the Visuddhimagga. Though these rules pertain to a certain group in a specific time and place, they have been used throughout the Muslim world and are themselves the basis for later Sufi instructional works. These rules give one of many variations on Sufi training. Many rules resonate with advice to Buddhist, Hindu, Kabbalist, and early Christian seekers. Just as the Bhakti is told to keep to satsang, al-Muridan advises: "The Sufi should associate with people of his kind and those from whom he can benefit." The novice should attach himself to a qualified teacher, or *shayk*, constantly seeking his direction and obeying him fully. He is urged to render service to his shayk and his fellows. Service is exalted as the best calling for the aspirant; the servant is said to rank next to the shayk himself. As in the Visuddhimagga and Christ's Sermon on the Mount, the novice's rules dictate: "One should not be concerned about the provisions of livelihood nor should one be occupied in seeking, gathering and storing them." For the Prophet himself "did not store anything for the morrow." Coveting food, clothes, or shelter hinders the Sufi's purity, for God revealed: "Those hearts which were bound to their desires were screened from Him." Though celibacy is not required of Sufis, these twelfth-century rules adjure: "In our times it is better to avoid marriage and suppress desire by discipline, hunger, vigils, and traveling." Finally, the Sufi

must be a Moslem par excellence, observing all rules of
the faith to the letter, for "the more saintly the man, the
more strictly will he be judged."

Each Sufi master, order, and group has its own
methods or combination of teaching techniques. The
ways vary, but the goal is the same. Mahmud Shabastri,
a master and author of *The Secret Garden*, put it this way:

> That man attains to the secret of unity
> Who is not detained at the stages on the road.
> Your being is naught but thorns and weeds,
> Cast it all clean away from you.
> Go sweep out the chamber of your heart,
> Make it ready to be the dwelling place of the
>   Beloved.
> When you depart out, He will enter in,
> In you, void of yourself, will He display
>   His beauty.

Sufi doctrine holds men are bound by their conditioning—the thorns and weeds that keep them from God.
The ordinary man is trapped in suffering by his conditioning. Strong habits of thought, feeling, and perception
dictate human reactions to the world; man is a slave to his
habits. People are asleep but do not know it. To awaken
them to their condition—the first step in escaping it—
people need a shock. One function of Sufi teaching
stories, such as the tale of the blind men and the ele-
phant, is to provide such a shock. These tales have many
layers of meaning. Some are hidden to most hearers,
some obvious. Not everyone gets the same lessons from
the stories, for what the listener hears depends on his
stage along the Sufi path. The skillful teacher uses just

the right tale at the perfect moment to impart an understanding for which the student is ripe.

Such shocks and lessons all help the Sufi aspirant on his way to inner purification. According to Sufi psychology, our habitual impulses are the stuff of the lower soul, or *nafs*, which must be disciplined and watched continually lest it lead the seeker toward evil and away from God. Al-Muridin recommends overcoming the influence of nafs by detached observation of its workings. Nafs, goes a saying, are like an idol; looking at it with sympathy is idolatry; looking with scrutiny is worship. Through detached scrutiny of his lower urges, impulses, and desires, the Sufi can break their hold over his mind and so replace his negative qualities with virtuous ones.

Al-Muridin comments in his rules that "the consummate Sufi is in a position of stability, and he is immune to the effects of the changeful states of mind or harsh circumstances." This equanimity allows the finished Sufi to be in the world but not of it. A calm exterior, however, may not reflect the inner ecstasy of a close communion with God. One modern shayk describes the Sufi's supreme state as "being inwardly drunk and outwardly sober."

One old master includes in his list of the finished Sufi's attributes: a sense of being subject entirely to God rather than one's own will; the desire to have no personal desire; "grace"—that is, perfect performance of acts in God's service; truthfulness in thought and deed; putting others' interests before one's own; service with complete self-disregard; constant remembrance of God; generosity, fearlessness, and the ability to die nobly. But Sufis may balk at such specific formulae for measuring spiritual progress, or worse, at trying to gauge another's attainments through such a checklist.

Those who would judge others should heed the advice in a Sufi tale retold by Idries Shah (1971: p. 75):

Yaqub, the son of the Judge, said that one day he questioned Bahaudin Nawshband in this manner: When I was in companionship with the Murshid of Tabriz, he regularly made a sign that he was not to be spoken to, when he was in a condition of special reflection. But you are accessible to us at all times. Am I correct in concluding that this difference is due to your undoubtedly greater capacity of detachment, the capacity being under your dominion, rather than fugitive?
Bahaudin told him:
No, you are always seeking comparisons between people and between states. You are always seeking evidences and differences, when you are not you are seeking similarities. You do not really need so much explanation in matters which are outside such measurement. Different modes of behavior on the part of the wise are to be regarded as due to differences in individuality; not of quality.

8. TRANSCENDENTAL MEDITATION

Transcendental Meditation (TM) is the best-known meditation technique in the West and Maharishi Mahesh Yogi, its formulator, the most famous yogi. TM is a classic Hindu mantra meditation in a modern Western package. Maharishi has been artful in his avoidance of

Sanskrit terms and use of scientific findings to validate meditation in a skeptical culture so that normal Americans can feel comfortable joining in a practice developed by and for Hindus in India. He also downplays the orthodox nature of his beliefs. The theory behind TM— "Science of Creative Intelligence"—is an updated restatement of the basic teaching of Sankaracharya's eighth-century Advait school of Vedantic thought.

Sankaracharya wrote at a time when Buddhism dominated India. His highly successful religious crusade revived Hinduism, offering a final state of nonduality rather than nirvana to the seeker. The goal of Advait is union of the seeker's mind with the formless Brahma or infinite consciousness, a step beyond the Bhakti's goal of union with a form of God. The means to this formless union is samadhi. This is also the goal in TM, though Maharishi no longer describes it in these terms. TM traces its root back to Sankaracharya, though it is a reformulation of Advait thought tailored to Western ears.

Maharishi's technique of TM is in the mainstream of jhana practices, though it is often touted as unique. Like all Advait yogis, Maharishi sees that "duality is the fundamental cause of suffering." His technique for transcending duality begins with repetition of a mantra, a Sanskrit word or sound. Just as in the Visuddhimagga, in which different meditation subjects are given to people of different temperament, Maharishi claims that selection of the proper mantra for a particular individual is a vital factor in TM. And just as the Visuddhimagga depicts finer levels of one-pointedness as increasingly blissful and sublime, Maharishi describes the increasing "charm" as the mind is allowed to follow its natural tendency to go to "a field of greater happiness" by entering the subtler states of a thought—that is, the mantra.

There is a mystique about the specialness of each person's mantra, and teachers admonish newcomers never to reveal theirs to anyone or even speak it aloud. But as meditators are sometimes chagrined to learn, people who fall into general categories of age, education, and so on, are given the same mantra. The mantras themselves are by no means special to TM but come from standard Sanskrit sources used by many Hindus today. Like millions of modern Bhaktis in India, the TM meditator in Des Moines may be silently intoning "Shyam" (a name of Lord Krishna), or "Aing" (a sound sacred to the Divine Mother).

The beliefs that particular mantric sounds bestow certain boons or are appropriate to special types of persons is widespread in Hinduism. The ancient *Saiva Upanishads*, for example, contain a discourse on the fifty letters of the Sanskrit alphabet, treating each as a mantra in itself and describing its special virtues. The letter *umkara* (Ū) gives strength; *kumkara* (kā) is an antidote against poisons; *ghamkara* (gha) bestows prosperity; *phamkara* (pha) grants psychic powers.

In TM, meditators learn to avoid effortful concentration. The student is told to bring his mind gently back to the mantra as it wanders. In effect, this process is one of becoming one-pointed, though concentration is passive rather than forced. The following oft-quoted description by Maharishi (1969: p. 470) of the nature of TM well describes the focal narrowing of attention on a meditation object, and transcendence of the object, in ascending through access concentration to the second jhana. Transcendental meditation, he says, entails ". . . turning the attention inward towards the subtler levels of a thought until the mind transcends the experience of the subtlest state of the thought ,nd arrives at the source of thought . . ."

As in the jhanas, bliss arises with the stillness of mind. The goal of mantra is what Maharishi calls "transcendental consciousness": when mind "arrives at the direct experience of bliss, it loses all contact with the outside and is contented in the state of transcendental bliss-consciousness." In the language of the Visuddhimagga, this is access concentration or jhana. The next phase in Maharishi's program is the infusion of jhana, or transcendental consciousness, into the waking, dreaming, and sleeping states by alternating normal activity with periods of meditation. The state thereby achieved he calls "cosmic consciousness" in which "no activity, however rigorous, can take one out of Being." Maharishi denies the need to impose renunciation on oneself. He sees purification as part of cosmic consciousness. It is an effect of transcendence, not a prerequisite. According to Maharishi, "Proficiency in the virtues can only be gained by repeated experience of samadhi."

Before the meditator gains cosmic consciousness, the effects of his daily meditation gradually wear off as time passes; in cosmic consciousness, these effects persist always. Maharishi elaborates the transition from transcendental to cosmic consciousness (1966: p. 53):

From this state of pure Being the mind comes back again to experience the thought in the relative world . . . With more and more practice, the ability of the mind to maintain its essential nature while experiencing objects through the senses increases. When this happens the mind and its essential nature, the state of transcendental Being, become one, and the mind is then capable of retaining its essential nature—Being—while engaged in thought, speech or action.

He sees cosmic consciousness as a state in which two distinct levels of organization in nervous system function. Usually, these levels inhibit each other, but here they operate side by side while they maintain their unique characteristics: Transcendental consciousness, for example, co-exists with the waking state. "Silence," says Maharishi, "is experienced with activity and yet is separate from it." The meditator in cosmic consciousness finds this inner peace persists in all circumstances as a "pure awareness" along with activity. Although the effects of transcendence during meditation can wear off after meditation is over, once mastered, cosmic consciousness is permanent. The person in cosmic consciousness has experienced in transcendence a jhanic state in which sense perception ceases. During waking, he remains relatively detached from sense perception, although he is more sensitive to both his own thought processes and external events.

As cosmic consciousness deepens, the meditator finds the bliss of transcendental consciousness persisting now in other states. As this bliss pervades other areas of his life, he finds that by comparison sensual pleasures are not so enchanting as before. While he still has desires, his actions are no longer driven by them. His state is one of equanimity: The turbulence and excitement of intense emotions—fear, grief, anger, depression, or craving—are softened by a permanent state of "restful alertness." Finally, they cease to arise. Equanimity also shows up in the meditator better resisting the fluctuating pull of life stress and daily tensions. He finds a new inner steadiness prevails, whereas once he would have wavered. Even-mindedness also manifests in the meditator loving others in equal share without undue fondness for specific people; his attachments weaken. He also finds he is more easily contented with whatever comes, more free from desires and dislikes. According to Maharishi, life in cosmic consciousness is tensionless. (1969: p. 287):

> . . . the enlightened man lives a life of fulfillment. His actions, being free from desire, serve only the need of the time. He has no personal interest to gain. He is engaged in fulfilling the cosmic purpose and therefore his actions are guided by nature. This is why he does not have to worry about his needs. His needs are the needs of nature, which takes care of their fulfillment, he being the instrument of the Divine.

A further step in the progression promised by Maharishi is God consciousness. This state is the result of devotion while in cosmic consciousness. In "God consciousness" the meditator perceives all things as sacred; "everything is naturally experienced in the awareness of God." At first, says Maharishi, this experience of unity in diversity can be overwhelming, and the meditator can become deeply lost in it. Gradually, however, God consciousness mixes with other activities, just as at an earlier stage transcendental consciousness merged with normal states to produce cosmic consciousness.

In God consciousness the meditator surrenders his individuality. This is "the most purified state" in which the meditator has overcome the least stain of impurity in thought or deed; he now dwells in perfect harmony with nature and the divine. Arriving at God consciousness, ac-

cording to Maharishi, entails a transformation, whereby
one is aware of God in all aspects of creation. Beyond
God consciousness the TM devotee may evolve into a
state called "unity." Here his consciousness is so refined
that he perceives all things free of any conceptual illu-
sion.

The means to these higher states in TM are advanced
techniques given to meditators over the course of several
years of practice and of service to the TM organization.
Though TM spokesmen may vaguely acknowledge these
more advanced methods, they never divulge their specifics. While the popular impression is that mantra meditation is the whole of TM, it seems that the meditator
must learn these secret, advanced practices in order to
reach the higher states described in the Science of Creative Intelligence.

9. PATANJALI'S
ASHTANGA YOGA

The manual for meditators closest to the Visuddhimagga
in Hinduism is Patanjali's *Yoga Sutras*, still the most au-
thoritative source on yoga today (Prabhavananda and
Isherwood, 1969; Vivekananda, 1970.) Most every modern Indian meditation system, including TM, acknowledges the Yoga Sutras as one source of their own
method. There are numerous spiritual schools called
"yoga": Bhakti yoga is the path of devotion; karma yoga
uses selfless service; and gyana yoga takes the intellect as
its vehicle. The path outlined in the Yoga Sutras sub-
sumes them all.

Though their means may differ, all yogic paths seek to transcend duality in union. All these paths see the locus of duality as within the mind, in the separation between the mechanisms of awareness and their object. To transcend duality, the seeker must enter a state in which this gap is bridged, the experiencer and the object merging. This state is samadhi, in which the meditator's awareness merges with its contents.

The yoga aphorisms are a skeletal map to this state. The mind, it explains, is filled with thought waves that create the gulf that yoga seeks to bridge. By calming his thought waves, by stilling his mind, the yogi will find union. These thought waves are the source of strong emotions and blind habits that bind man to a false self. When his mind becomes clear and still, man can know himself as he really is. In this stillness, he can know God. In the process, his mistaken belief in himself as a separate, unique individual apart from God will be overcome. As his thought waves are subdued, the yogi's ego recedes. Finally, as a liberated man, he is able to don his ego or discard it like a suit of clothes. Donning the ego, he acts in the world; discarding it by stilling his mind, he unites with God.

But first he must undergo an arduous discipline of mind and body. This transformation begins with concentration, bringing his mind to one-pointedness. In Patanjali's system, one-pointedness is the main method around which all others turn. Some sources date the Aphorisms back more than fifteen hundred years, to about the same period as the Visuddhimagga. The spiritual *Zeitgeist* of that era is reflected in both; indeed, the paths they outline are in large part identical. The main difference between these two meditation manuals is Patanjali's insistence that samadhi rather than nirvana is the highway to liberation.

The royal, or *raja*, yoga outlined by Patanjali entails *ashtanga:* eight key practices or limbs. The first two, *yama* and *niyama*, are moral training for purity. The next two are *asana*, the development through physical exercises of a firm and erect posture, or "seat," and *pranayam*, exercises for controlling and stilling the breath. Both the third and fourth limbs have become intricately developed in their own right, so that some yogic schools use these practices as their main methods—and most Americans associate "yoga" exclusively with these two limbs.

Most textbooks of *hatha* and pranayam point out that these are helps to the attainment of samadhi, not ends in themselves. Some, however, focus solely on rigorous physical purifications as means to alter consciousness. Vyas Dev (1970), for example, details 250 *asana* postures, elaborates fifty different pranayam exercises and twenty-five *shat-karmas* and *mudras*—methods for cleansing internal organs. Before sitting in deep meditation for a long time, advises Vyas Dev, the yogi should clear his bowels completely by drawing in and expelling water through his anus, empty his bladder by drawing in water and then expelling it through a catheter, and purify his digestive system by swallowing and extracting about seventy feet of string made of fine yarn. He should also swallow two or three pints of lukewarm salt water to make himself vomit and swallow and extract a three-inch-wide strip of cloth seven yards long to finish the job. Then he is ready for serious meditation.

Patanjali's stipulation about these first four limbs, however, is that the yogi should do them simply to the point at which his body and mind are stilled. These are mere preliminaries for sitting in meditation, useful for overcoming the obstacles to concentration such as doubt, sloth, despair, and craving for sensual pleasures. Actual meditation begins with the second group of limbs. These are all steps in becoming one-pointed. In the fifth limb, *pratyahara*, the yogi withdraws his mind from sense objects, focusing his attention on the meditation object. In the sixth, *dharana*, he holds his mind on the object. The seventh, *dhyana*, involves "an unbroken flow of thought toward the object of concentration." The sixth and seventh limbs correspond to initial and sustained application of attention in the Visuddhimagga system. The final limb is samadhi.

The combination dharana, dhyana, and samadhi is a state called *samyama*. This highly concentrated state holds the key to supernormal powers such as clairvoyance and telepathy. The Sutras have a lengthy section on how to apply samyama to gain various powers. By focusing samyama on his memories, the yogi can retrieve knowledge of his past lives; samyama on the marks of another's body reveals his state of mind; samyama on the yogi's own throat stills his hunger and thirst. As in the Visuddhimagga, the Sutras see these powers as subtle snares for the seeker. The yogi is urged to give up these seductive traps as last temptations for the ego.

The aphorisms say that samyama on "single moments and their sequence" gives discriminative knowledge, or *prajna*, which "delivers from the bondage of ignorance." But this foray into the path of insight seems glossed over in most modern commentaries on Patanjali. It is samadhi that is taught as the heart of yoga; Vivekananda (1970) says, "samadhi is Yoga proper; that is the highest means." Patanjali lists many suitable objects for concentration: the syllable Om, or other mantra; the heart; a deity or "illumined soul"; or a divine symbol. The yogi, in merging consciousness with the primary object, will first achieve savichara samadhi—access concentration. In this level of samadhi, there is identity with the primary object "mixed with awareness of name, quality, and knowledge." After this comes *nirvichara* samadhi—first jhana, in which there is identity without other awareness. Once the nirvichara level is gained, the yogi is to wipe out even the thought of the primary object and so attain *nirvikalpa* samadhi (as in the example of Sri Ramakrishna), in which all sense of duality is obliterated.

Nirvikalpa is the deepest samadhi; in it, mind is at its stillest. Yogic lore has it that one in this state could remain for as long as three months in continuous deep meditation, his breath and other metabolic functions virtually suspended all that time. In this samadhi, says one commentator, "an avalanche of indescribable bliss sweeps away all relative ideas of pain and blame . . . All doubts and misgivings are quelled forever; the oscillations of mind are stopped; the momentum of past actions is exhausted." But one limit of nirvikalpa samadhi is that it can be enjoyed only while the yogi remains still, absorbed in deep meditation.

The final step in ashtanga yoga is extending the deep stillness of samadhi into the yogi's waking state. When samadhi spreads throughout other states so that no activity or inner stirring can dislodge its hold on the yogi's mind, this marks him as a *jivan-mukti*, a liberated man. In his introduction to Sri Ramakrishna's biography, the anonymous chronicler gives an eloquent account of the state enjoyed by that saint (M., 1928: p. 27). On emerging from nirvikalpa samadhi:

> he is devoid of ideas of "I" and "mine," he looks on the body as a mere shadow, an outer sheath encasing the soul. He does not dwell on the past, takes no thought for the future, and looks with indifference

on the present. He surveys everything in the world
with an eye of equality; he is no longer touched by
the infinite variety of phenomenon; he no longer
reacts to pleasure and pain. He remains unmoved
where he—that is to say, his body—is worshipped
by the good or tormented by the wicked; for he realizes that it is the one Brahman that manifests itself
through everything.

The Indian saint Ramana Maharshi (1962) proposed a
simple operational definition for distinguishing between a
yogi in nirvikalpa samadhi and one in sahaj samadhi: If
there remains a difference between samadhi and the waking state, it is nirvikalpa samadhi at best; if no difference,
the yogi has reached his goal of sahaj samadhi.

The yogi in sahaj partially resides in samadhi, no
longer identifying with his thoughts or senses. His being
is grounded in a consciousness transcending the sensory
world, and so he remains detached from that world while
operating in it. This "ideal of Yoga, the state of *jivan-
mukti*," writes Eliade (1970), is life in an "eternal present"
in which one "no longer possesses a personal consciousness—that is, a consciousness nourished on his own history—but a witness consciousness which is pure lucidity
and spontaneity."

In sahaj samadhi, meditation is a self-sustained, spontaneous fact of the yogi's existence. He expresses his
stillness of mind in his actions. He is free of all ego ties
and interests; his actions are no longer bound by the de-
posits of the past. Meher Baba (1967) describes this as "a
state of full wakefulness in which there is no ebb and
flow, waxing or waning, but only the steadiness of true
perception." The jivan-mukti has transcended his body
consciousness along with the conceptual universe; he

does not see the world as different from himself. For one who dwells in sahaj, there is no ego, and there are no "others."

10. INDIAN TANTRA AND KUNDALINI YOGA

The Tantric tradition native to India is, according to some sources, a refinement of ancient shamanistic practices that has found its way into both Hindu and Buddhist meditation systems (Eliade, 1970). Indian Tantra alters consciousness by arousing energies that are normally latent. Some meditation systems introduced to the West have their roots in "kundalini" yoga, a Tantric teaching. Kundalini, says Tantric physiology, is a huge reserve of spiritual energy located at the base of the spine. When aroused, kundalini travels up the spine through six centers, or *"chakras,"* reaching the seventh at the top of the head. Kundalini has few specific correlates with Western notions of anatomy. Chakras refer to energy patterns, localized in certain physical centers.

When kundalini focuses in a chakra, it activates characteristic energies of these centers. Each chakra has an emblematic set of attitudes, motives, and mental states that dominate a person's mind when kundalini sparks it. The first chakra, located between the anus and the genitals, involves the struggle to survive. Territoriality, possessiveness, brute force, undue preoccupation with the body and health, and fear for one's safety all reflect the mental state of the first chakra. The second chakra embodies sexuality and sensuality. It is in the genitals. When this chakra is active, lust, greed, and craving for sensual delights are one's predominant states of mind. The urge to be powerful and influence others is tied to the third chakra, located near the navel. Persuasion or manipulation of others to serve one's own ends are third-chakra behavior.

Most people much of the time are motivated by mental states in which these first three chakras are active. Kundalini yoga aims to bring this energy up to the higher chakras, just as Kabbalah seeks to raise consciousness to higher planes. The fourth chakra, in the center of the chest by the heart, represents selfless love and caring for others. The pure love of a mother for her child is of the fourth chakra. But fourth-chakra love is not romantic; rather, it combines with a clear-sighted detachment to make for compassion. When kundalini activates the three topmost chakras, the yogi experiences transcendental states. These three centers are the fifth chakra at the throat, the sixth at the center of the forehead, and the seventh at the top of the head. The meditator seeks to free kundalini from his lower chakras, in which it ordinarily is trapped, and raise it to his higher ones. When it reaches his seventh chakra and stabilizes there, he feels a state of intense ecstasy and union with God. He is considered liberated, free of bondage to those habits and acts stemming from the lower chakras by which most men are bound.

The essence of Tantric practice is the use of the senses to transcend sense consciousness in samadhi. Though the senses are, of course, the means to transcendence in all techniques for one-pointedness, Tantrism is unique in the diversity of techniques it offers for transcending sense consciousness. Among them are the use of mantra;

yantra, objects for visualization exercises such as a man-
dala; concentration on *shabd*, supersubtle inner sounds;
pranayam and asanas; concentration on the play of forces
in the chakras; and *maithuna*, the arousal of *shakti*—
kundalini energy—through controlled, ritual sexual intercourse.

Maithuna is the Tantric technique that most fascinates
Westerners, who more often than not mistake it for an
indulgence of sexual appetites rather than a means to
their mastery. Ritual intercourse is a potent means to
arouse kundalini energy, allowing the self-disciplined
yogi to raise this energy to his higher chakras. Maithuna
is one of five actions generally prohibited to Hindu yogis
but used by Tantrics of the Bon Marg, or "left-handed
path." The first four are imbibing fish, meat, liquor, and
performing certain mudras, all of which the Tantric does
in a strictly prescribed manner, as a prelude to maithuna.
Throughout the ritual, he does silent japa of his own
special mantra, given by his guru, and at points he recites certain other mantras. During maithuna itself, the
yogi carries out carefully delineated ritual actions—
including exactly where and how to touch his partner's
body.

In maithuna, the male is passive, the female active;
since the arousal of energy rather than climax is the goal,
there is little movement. During intercourse, the Tantric
mentally recites mantras such as "Om, thou goddess re-
splendent . . . into the fire of the self, using the mind as
a sacrificial ladle, I, who am engaged in harnessing the
sense organs, offer this oblation." At the moment of ejac-
ulation, he is to repeat a mantra that consecrates his
semen itself as a sacrificial offering (Bharati, 1970). The
key to maithuna, as well as the goal of all Tantric practices, is the detachment borne of samadhi. This detach-

ment converts the energy of desires into higher forms. Tantric texts frequently repeat (Eliade, 1970: p. 263): "By the same acts that cause some men to burn in hell for thousands of years, the Yogin gains his eternal salvation."

Tantric language is veiled and so is open to many levels of interpretation. Actions that from outside seem improper can have within Tantra a special, deeper meaning. An example of this double meaning in Tantra is a Tibetan *kapala*, a cup made of human skull mounted on a silver stand. Its description in a museum reads:

> The vessel holds the Amrit used for performing esoteric rituals. Those who have such dualistic concepts as the clean and the unclean cannot think of using a human skull. But the Tantrics, who have gained Transcendental Wisdom, have no superstition and to them golden cups and human skulls are the same. The skulls are used to symbolize this attitude of mind.

One modern version of kundalini yoga is *siddha-yoga*, taught by Swami Muktananda (Amma, 1969; Muktananda, 1969, 1970). This system begins with traditional practices such as asana, pranayam, chanting, and japa. He instructs the beginner to meditate with the mantra, "Guru Om," or with each breath, "so-ham." Muktananda emphasizes the guru-disciple relationships. The core of siddha-yoga training is the tradition in which the guru grants a direct, instantaneous transcendental experience to the devotee. This process, called *shaktipat diksha*, is an initiation by look, touch, or word. In this transmission the devotee who approaches the guru with love, devotion, and faith has his shakti—the energy of kundalini—aroused.

When this happens, all other practices can fall away. The inner action of kundalini produces spontaneous meditation, pranayam, asanas, and mudras without the devotee's prior training or volition. This process of puri- fication through shaktipat is said to take three to twelve years. In this period it transforms the entire personality of the devotee, the "limited I" having been abandoned. The devotee attains a sense of "oneness with all-pervad- ing Cosmic Intellect." The imagery and terminology with which Muktananda describes this process is that of kundalini (1970: p. 54):

> . . . . the Kundalini, which stays in the *Muladhara,* gradually travels upwards piercing the chakras on her way until she reaches *Sahasrara,* the thousand-pet- alled lotus in the crown of the head . . . and the spiritual endeavor of an aspirant gets fulfilled.

During shaktipat the meditator may experience a wide variety of involuntary reactions. These include powerful moods of joy, dullness, or agitation; strange bodily pos- tures, gestures, tremors, or dancing poses; feelings of wonder or fright; a period of pain in all parts of the body; various internal stirrings, muscle throbbing or thrills; spontaneous deep meditation; visions of lights, deities, or celestial places accompanied by a great joy and bliss; and, finally, there is a "divine light of indescribable lustre" or a subtle inner sound during meditation (Muktananda, 1970).

These phenomena serve to purify the meditator so that he can sustain *turiya*—a state akin to jhana—while in the three ordinary states of waking, dreaming, and sleeping. He reaches the further state of *Turiyatita* when his kun- dalini has stabilized in the topmost chakra, the *sahasrara.*

A person in this advanced state has forgotten body consciousness, enjoys extraordinary bliss and profound tranquility, and has attained "the fruit of Yoga," remaining "ever absorbed in the Supreme State," whatever he does. He performs any and all acts with peace and equanimity. A disciple of Muktananda, Amma (1969: p. 11), says of one in this state, "He has nothing to do and nothing to achieve; still he does the activities of worldly life remaining a witness to them all." One in turiyatita has become a siddha, a name denoting the supernormal psychic powers he is said to possess, among which is the capability of raising kundalini in others.

Tantra yoga alone among traditional meditation systems sees the yogi's attainment of *siddhis*, or supernormal psychic powers, as marking the end of his path. Says one Tantric scripture, "For all sadhana ceases when it has borne its fruit in siddhi." Certain Tantric practices are devised to produce certain siddhis such as mind reading. One reason siddhis may signify liberation for some is the high states that the possession of powers betokens. But meditation is central to all Tantric practices; the raising of kundalini, the means; samadhi, the goal.

11. TIBETAN BUDDHISM

The techniques of Tibetan Mahayana are founded in the classical Buddhist tradition that the Visuddhimagga expresses. It also blends with the classical, purely Tibetan elements and Tantraism. In an outline of meditation theory and practice by the Dalai Lama (1965), the theory

presented is essentially that of the Theravadan Visuddhimagga—or as Mahayanists call Theravada, the "Hinayana" tradition, or "Lesser Vehicle," in contrast to their
"Greater Vehicle." A critical difference between these
two main Buddhist traditions is the Mahayana bodhisattva vow to gain enlightenment not just for oneself but
for the sake of the salvation of all sentient beings. This
difference in motive, says the Dalai Lama, is decisive; it
makes a difference in both path and goal. He sees the
hinayana nirvana as a prior stage to the Mahayana goal of
bodhisattvahood. Still, his conception of the nirvanic
state agrees with the Visuddhimagga: it is "liberation
from this bondage" of *samsara* by a cessation in which the
"roots of delusion are thoroughly extracted," the ego or
"I-thought" severed. But for Mahayanists the goal is
beyond nirvana, in returning to the world and helping
others toward salvation.

Motive makes the difference between where insight
into emptiness brings the meditator. If he developed insight solely to liberate himself, he will be what, as we
have seen earlier, the Visuddhimagga calls an *"arahant."*
If he was motivated by the "Bodhi-chitta of love and
compassion," he gains the "superior release" of the bodhisattva, in which his state of consciousness makes him a
more perfect vehicle of compassion so he can lead others
toward liberation. In either case, says the Dalai Lama, a
bodhisattva has "cleansed his mind of all impurities and
has removed the motives and inclinations that lead to
them." He has severed ties to the normal world of name
and form, the locus of ordinary consciousness.

The Mahayana path begins with a close cousin of the
Visuddhimagga teaching. There are three "moral precepts," ways for the meditator to realize the "Triple Refuge"—Buddha, Dharma, and Sangha—as his internal

realities. The Tibetan Buddhist meditator's first precept is sila, vows of upright behavior. The second is samadhi (Tibetan: *shiney*), fixing the mind on one object to develop his one-pointedness. The recommended conditions in which to practice samadhi are as in the Visuddhimagga. The meditator should go into seclusion, sever his ties to worldly activities, and so on. The early meditation objects include those listed in the Visuddhimagga, such as mindfulness of the breath. Some, especially in later stages, resemble Indian Tantric deities. These more advanced subjects are the object of visualization. Such subjects come in innumerable aspects "so that they suit the physical, mental and sensuous attitudes of different individuals," and arouse strong faith and devotion. These visualization subjects embody different aspects of the mind. The meditator identifies with these mental states or qualities as he visualizes the figure. Chogyam Trungpa (1975: p. 47) describes one such figure:

On the disc of the autumn moon, clear and pure, you place a seed syllable. The cool blue rays of the seed syllable emanate immense cooling compassion that radiates beyond the limits of sky or space. It fulfills the needs and desires of sentient beings, bringing basic warmth so that confusions may be clarified. Then from the seed syllable you create a Mahavairocana Buddha, white in color, with the features of an aristocrat—an eight-year-old child with a beautiful, innocent, pure, powerful, royal gaze. He is dressed in the costume of a medieval king of India. He wears a glittering gold crown inlaid with wishfulfilling jewels. Part of his long black hair floats over his shoulders and back; the rest is made into a topknot surmounted by a glittering blue dia-

mond. He is seated crosslegged on the lunar disc
with his hands in the meditation mudra holding a
vajra carved from pure white crystal.

The Dalai Lama lists four steps in reaching samadhi.
There is an initial fixing of the meditator's mind on the
primary object while he tries to prolong his period of
concentration on it. In the next stage, his concentration is
intermittent. Distractions come and go in his mind, alternating with attention to the primary object. At this stage,
he may experience joy and ecstasy arising from his one-
pointedness; these feelings will strengthen his efforts at
concentration. This stage, like jhana access, culminates
when his mind finally overcomes all disturbances, ena-
bling him to concentrate on the object without any inter-
ruption whatsoever in the perfect one-pointedness of the
jhanas. The final stage is that of "mental quiescence," in
which his total concentration comes with minimal effort—that is, jhana mastery. The meditator can now concentrate on any object with effortless ease; psychic powers have become possible.

Jhana mastery matters in Mahayana not because of the
powers made possible but due to its usefulness in the
meditator's realizing "*Sunyata*," the essential emptiness of
the phenomenal world, including the world within the
meditator's own mind. The means for this breakthrough
is the meditator's third precept, the practice of vipassana
(Tibetan: *thagthong*). He uses the power of samadhi as a
steppingstone for meditation on Sunyata. The Dalai
Lama (1965) does not specify details of vipassana technique in Tibetan practice. But he does mention that the
flow of the meditator's undisciplined mind can be
stopped "and the wandering or projecting mind brought
to rest by concentration on the physical makeup of one's

body and the psychological makeup of one's mind"—two techniques of vipassana taught in the Visuddhimagga. By means of vipassana with Sunyata as focus, the meditator discards his ego beliefs, finally reaching "the goal that leads to the destruction of all moral and mental defilements."

This goal does not, however, represent the culmination of the meditator's spiritual development in Tibetan Buddhism but a stage along the way in his further practice and evolution. The control of mental processes he gains through concentration and insight prepare him for further training in techniques such as visualizations and the cultivation of qualities such as compassion. The many schools within Tibetan Buddhism each has its particular emphasis and unique program for advanced training. In all of them, the basic meditative skills of concentration and insight are prerequisites for more complex, advanced efforts in training the meditator's mind.

Chogyam Trungpa (1976), in summarizing the Tibetan Buddhist path, advises that before the meditator begins any advanced Tibetan techniques, he needs to develop "transcendental common sense, seeing things as they are." For this reason, vipassana meditation forms the meditator's foundation. With his seeing things clearly, the meditator relaxes his defenses in his daily living situation. This opens him to *shunyata*, "direct experience without any props." This, in turn, inspires the meditator to aim toward the bodhisattva ideal. But this is not the end of the path: Beyond the bodhisattva experience is that of the "yogi," beyond the yogi is the "siddha," and beyond the siddha lies the "Buddha." At each of these levels, the seeker has a unique sense of himself and the world—for example, the bodhisattva experiences shunyata. At a still higher level is the psychological space of *mahamudra.* Here, says Trungpa (Guenther and Trungpa, 1975: p. 36), "symbols do not exist as such; the sense of experience ceases to exist. Directly relating to the play of situations, energy develops through a movement of spontaneity that never becomes frivolous." This leads one to "destroy whatever needs to be destroyed, and foster whatever needs to be fostered." When one has arrived at mahamudra, there is no more struggling along the path.

It is difficult for someone to assess the true nature of any spiritual path without himself participating in its practices. This applies all the more to systems like Tibetan Buddhism in which the heart of instruction is esoteric. Vajrayana, the tantric segment of Tibetan Buddhism, is veiled in secrecy; the great legendary tantric Milarepa warns (Chang, 1970): "The teachings of Tantra should be practiced secretly; they will be lost if demonstrated in the marketplace." Even if told publicly, many Tibetan methods are "self-secret" so that one needs to practice them and experience their fruits truly to understand them. Translations like Evans-Wentz' (1968, 1969) give the reader a vivid taste of Tibetan teachings. But to follow this intricate path, one needs to find a lama as guru, for even now specific methods in Tibetan Buddhism are transmitted only from teacher to student in teaching lineages that date back centuries.

12. ZEN

The word "Zen" is a cognate of the Pali word *jhana*, and both derive from the Sanskrit dhyana (meditation). The cultural interchange that culminated in Japanese Zen links to the Visuddhimagga tradition through the Ch'an meditation school of China. The changes undergone in the voyage through time and space from India of the fifth century to Japan of the present day are more evident in doctrine than in the specifics of practice. Doctrinal differences—much like those between Theravada and Mahayana Buddhism—have emphasized these changes and obscured the similarities. Some versions of Zen meditation, or *zazen*, remain identical to mindfulness or insight. As with mindfulness, all varieties of zazen broaden their focus from sitting meditation to the meditator's whole range of life situations.

Zen's down-to-earth zazen matters, but extensive scriptural studies are discouraged. The early Soto master Dogen (1971: p. 62) stated:

> No matter how well you say you know . . . the esoteric and exoteric doctrines, as long as you possess a mind that clings to the body, you will be vainly counting others' treasures, without gaining even half a cent for yourself.

Zazen begins, as does vipassana, with a firm grounding in concentration; a wide variety of concentration techniques are employed. Samadhi or jhana is, in Zen terminology, the "great fixation" or "a state of oneness" in which the differences between things dissolve so that they appear to the meditator in the aspect of sameness. This is an intermediate stage on the path toward Zen's final realization. Suzuki warns (1958: p. 135): "When this state of great fixation is held as final, there will be no upturning, no outburst of satori, no penetration, no insight into Reality, no severing the bonds of birth and death."

Deep absorptions are not enough. They are necessary but not sufficient steps toward enlightenment. The wisdom of insight follows after and flows from samadhi.

Among Zen techniques are some unique methods for achieving jhana. One such, the *koan* (used primarily by the Rinzai sect), is a puzzle utterly impervious to solution by reason. Its "solution" lies in transcending thought by liberating the meditator's mind from the snare of language (Miura and Sasaki, 1965). Assigned a koan such as "What was your face before you were born?" or "What is Mu?" the aspirant keeps the koan constantly in mind. No matter what he is doing, when other matters intrude on his mind, he immediately lets them go and returns to his koan. As he discovers that his rational mind is unable to solve the insoluble, he reaches a feverish pitch of concentration from which arises a supreme frustration. As this happens, what once was a fully stated koan reduces to an emblematic fragment, for example, simply "Mu." When his discursive faculty finally exhausts itself, the moment of "realization" comes to the meditator. His thought ceases and he enters the state of *daigi*, or "fixation." His koan "yields up all its secrets" as he attains samadhi. (Suzuki, 1958).

Yasutani, a modern roshi who came to teach in America, utilized the koan for his more advanced students. He assigned beginners concentration on breathing. He saw as the aim of zazen not rendering the mind inactive in jhana but "quieting and unifying it in the midst of activity." Consequently, his students practiced concentration techniques until they developed a modicum of *joriki*, mental strength arising from one-pointedness of mind. The fruits of joriki are equanimity, determination, and a potential ripeness in the student for *Kensho-godo*, the *satori* awakening of "seeing into your True-nature."

When the student uses a koan, for instance, his samadhi comes to fruition when there is "absolute unity with Mu, unthinking absorption in Mu—this is ripeness." At this point, "inside and outside merge into a single unity." With this samadhi experience, *Kensho-godo* can take place, where he will "see each thing just as it is." A given *kensho* experience may fall anywhere within a wide range of depth, degree, and clarity.

Joriki strengthens the meditator's satori. This helps him extend his awakening beyond the session of zazen per se. The joriki he develops in his zazen cultivates the satori effect until finally it shapes all the rest of his daily life. When the student gains some control over his mind via one-pointedness exercises like counting breath or has exhausted his rational mind with koan, Yasutani-roshi frequently set him to a more advanced method called *shikan-taza*, "just sitting." In this type of Zen meditation, the student marshals a heightened state of concentrated awareness with no primary object. He just sits, keenly aware of whatever goes on in and around him. He sits alert and mindful, free from points of view or discriminating thoughts, merely watching. This technique is quite similar to vipassana. A related practice is "mobile zazen," in which he enters fully into every action with total attention and clear awareness. This corresponds to "bare attention" as described in the Visuddhimagga. Kapleau (1967) has noted these close parallels and cites a key Pali Sutra on mindfulness as a "prescription" for zazen:

In what is seen there must be just the seen;
In what is sensed there must be just the sensed;
In what is thought there must be just the thought.

There are many kinds of "satori" in zazen practice, some of which may be experiences of jhana, some stages in the path of insight. Yasutani warns his students, for example, to ignore *makyo*, visions and intense sensations. He says these may arise when the student's ability to concentrate develops to a point within reach of kensho, just as similar phenomena may arise when the meditator approaches the access concentration level. Kapleau describes a "false satori" stage, sometimes called the "cave of Satan," in which the meditator experiences deep serenity and believes he has reached his final realization. Just as with the pseudo nirvana on the vipassana path, this pseudoemancipation must be broken through. The final drive toward enlightenment as described by Kapleau (1967: p. 13) also fits the stages just prior to nirvana on the path of vipassana: The meditator's efforts are "powered on the one hand by a painfully felt inner bondage—a frustration with life, a fear of death, or both— and on the other by the conviction that through satori one can gain liberation." Yasutani notes that satori usually follows a period of samadhi. In an essay on his own Zen training, D. T. Suzuki says of his first attainment of samadhi, on the koan Mu (1970: p. 10):

> But this samadhi is not enough. You must come out of that state, be awakened from it and that awakening is prajna. That moment of coming out of samadhi and seeing it for what it is—that is satori.

Zen teachers stress the need to ripen an initial satori through further meditation until it finally permeates the meditator's whole life. Such full fruition means a state of mind stilled beyond any need for further practice. Suzuki (1949) describes this final state of mind as one in which the facts of one's daily experience are taken as they come; all events come into the meditator's awareness and are received with nonreaction. This nonreaction, clarifies Blofeld (1962), "does not mean trance-like dullness, but a brilliantly clear state of mind in which the details of every phenomenon are perceived, yet without evaluation or attachment."

Hui Hai, an old Zen master, put it, "When things happen, make no response: Keep your minds from dwelling on anything whatsoever." The fourteenth-century Zen master Bassui advised that zazen is "no more than looking into one's own mind, neither despising nor cherishing the thoughts that arise." This neutral stance is both means and end in Zen. It should extend beyond sitting in zazen into the rest of the meditator's day. Ruth Sasaki (*Miura and Sasaki*, 1965: p. xi) elaborates:

> The experienced practicer of zazen does not depend upon sitting in quietude on his cushion. States of consciousness at first attained only in the meditation hall gradually become continuous, regardless of what other activities he may be engaged in.

In the final Zen stage of "no mind," the spontaneous clarity of satori manifests in all one's acts. Here means and ends coalesce; the posture of mindfulness is built into the meditator's consciousness as a full awareness devoid of self-consciousness. Having experienced the impermanence of all things, that "life is pain, that all forms are *ku*, empty or voidness," he ceases clinging to the phenomenal world yet continues to act.

In recognition of the depth of this transformation of personality, there is little emphasis in Zen on moral precepts. Rather than merely imposing precepts from the outside, their observance emerges from within as a by-product of the change in consciousness zazen can bring.

Thomas Merton (1965) points out that Zen teachings inherit the spirit of the Taoist Chuang Tzu, who wrote these words (p. 112):

> No drives, no compulsions,
> No needs, no attractions:
> Then your affairs
> Are under control.
> You are a free man.

13. GURDJIEFF'S
FOURTH WAY

The spiritual system George I. Gurdjieff (1877–1948) brought to the West after extensive travel in Asia meeting "remarkable men" is, in the words of his pupil Orage, the religious teachings of the East disguised "in a terminology which would not alienate the factual minds of Western thinkers." Ouspensky (1971), another student of Gurdjieff, calls this system an "esoteric school," not suited to mass tastes, which tells *how* to do what popular religions teach *has* to be done, that is, transform one's consciousness. Gurdjieff himself called it "the Fourth Way": not the traditional path of the fakir, monk, or yogi but the way of the "sly man" who does not retreat from the world in solitary meditation but works on his consciousness in the mirror of his relationships with people, animals, property, and ideas. At an advanced stage, the Gurdjieff student must share his acquired knowledge with others in order to advance still further, so numerous second-, third-, and fourth-generation Gurdjieff groups have developed, each with its own style and idiosyncrasies. Since Gurdjieff's original school made use of a great range of techniques, any given latter-day group of his Fourth Way may or may not use the methods discussed here, which are primarily Ouspensky's.

Gurdjieff says most people are "asleep," living a life of automatic response to stimulus. "Contemporary man," writes Gurdjieff (1971), "has gradually deviated from the natural type he ought to have represented . . . the perceptions and manifestations of the modern man . . . represent only the results of automatic reflexes of one or another part of his general entirety." Like the Buddha, Gurdjieff understands man's normal state to be one of suffering. Human beings, because we are unable to see the situation as it really is, remain dominated by egoism, animal passions such as fear, excitement, and anger, and the pursuit of pleasure. Suffering, however, can give us an urge toward freedom. The way to liberation is not by conventional notions of virtuous living but by an intentional program for self-transformation. The remedy Gurdjieff offers begins with self-observation. Kenneth Walker (1969: p. 206), who studied with Ouspensky and Gurdjieff, puts it thus:

> We are imprisoned within our own minds, and however far we extend them and however highly we decorate them we still remain within their walls. If we are ever to escape from our prisons, the first step must be that we should realize our true situation and at the same time see ourselves as we really are and not as we imagine ourselves to be. This can be done by holding ourselves in a state of passive awareness . . .

Walker here describes "self-remembering," a technique of deliberately dividing one's attention so as to direct a portion back on oneself. Within one's multiple, fluctuating selves, one establishes an awareness that only watches all the rest: the "observing I" or the "witness." At first there is great difficulty in coming to a stable observing I, the beginner constantly forgets to remember himself, and self-observation melts into his usual full identification with whichever "I" has reign over his mind at a given moment. But with persistence the beginner's self-remembering strengthens, for, in Ouspensky's words, "the more we appreciate our present psychological state of sleep, the more we appreciate the urgent need to change it." Self-remembering is like mindfulness. The psychological stance required in this method is self-directed detachment, as though one's own thoughts and acts were those of some other person with whom one is only slightly acquainted. Ouspensky (Walker, 1969: p. 40) instructs:

> Observe yourself very carefully and you will see that not *you* but *it* speaks within you, moves, feels, laughs, and cries in you, just as *it* rains, clears up and rains again outside you. Everything happens in you, and your first job is to observe and watch it happening.

When the student realizes there has been a lapse in his self-observation, he returns his wandering mind to the task of watching himself. Though various Gurdjieff circles use a range of techniques, these are most often subsidiary to self-remembering. The critical skill sought is the capacity to direct attention to self-observation. Ouspensky (1971) names both the samadhi trance state and the normal state of identifying that "imprisons man in some small part of himself" as antithetical to his goal. Just as with insight meditation, in self-remembering, the "distorting glasses of the personality" are abandoned in order to see oneself clearly. In self-remembering, like mindfulness and zazen, one acknowledges oneself in entirety without comment and without naming what is seen.

Another example of Gurdjieffian self-remembering exercises is to focus on one aspect of everyday behavior— for example, movements of the hands or facial gestures— witnessing it all day. Still another instruction for self-remembering is: "Wherever one is, whatever one does, remember one's own presence and notice always what one does." These instructions are parallel to those for mindfulness. The similarity between systems is possibly no accident. Both Gurdjieff and Ouspensky traveled in lands in which vipassana or similar techniques were taught precisely to learn such methods, and Gurdjieff was a great borrower, reshaper, and transmitter of Eastern teachings.

In the course of self-remembering, the student realizes (as on the path of insight) that his inner states are in constant flux and that there is no such thing as a permanent "I" within. He sees, instead, an internal cast of characters or "principal features." Each, in turn, dominates the stage and adds its idiosyncrasies to the shape of his personality. With self-observation, the multiplicity of these selves becomes apparent but then falls away. Through observing them, these selves lose their hold as the student ceases to identify with them. As he strengthens his observing I and remains detached from all the others, the student will "wake up." In waking up, he sacrifices his everyday selves. Walker describes this awakened state as "a sense of being present, of being there, of thinking, perceiving, feeling and moving with a certain degree of control and not just automatically." In this state, the witness crystallizes as a constant mental function. The student can see himself with full objectivity.

This order of self-knowledge is preliminary to the highest state, "objective consciousness." In this state, the student sees not only himself but everything else as well with full objectivity. Objective consciousness is the culmination of self-remembering. One's ordinary consciousness is not dislodged, but full objectivity is superimposed on it. This adds an "inner silence" and a liberating sense of distance from the continuing rumblings of the mind. One's experience of the world in objective consciousness is entirely altered; Walker (1969: pp. 47–48) describes this end state in Gurdjieff's training:

> The small limiting "self" of everyday life, the self which insists on its personal rights and separateness, is no longer there to isolate one from everything else, and in its absence one is received into a much wider order of existence . . . as the clamor of thought within dies down into the inner silence, an overwhelming sense of "being" takes its place . . . Such limiting concepts as "yours" or "mine," "his" or "hers" are meaningless . . . and even those old divisions of time into "before" and "after" have been drowned in the fathomless depth of an ever-present "now." So also has disappeared . . . the division between the subject and the object, the knower and the thing known.

Bennett (1973) gives seven levels of man in Gurdjieff's system, the last three of which are "liberated"; these final three are gradations of objective consciousness. As part of his transformation to objective consciousness, one attains liberation from arbitrary, irrational influences from internal and external sources, respectively. The liberated person at the sixth level, for example, is the same as "the bodhisattva of Mahayana Buddhism, or the great saints and *wadis* of Christianity and Islam. He is no longer concerned with his own personal welfare, but has committed himself to the salvation of all creatures."

14. KRISHNAMURTI'S CHOICELESS AWARENESS

J. Krishnamurti, born in South India in the 1890s, was educated in England under the guidance of theosophist Annie Besant. Krishnamurti's view of the human predicament is close to that of Buddhism. The mind and the world, says Krishnamurti, are in everlasting flux: "There is only one fact, impermanence." The human mind clings to a "me" in the face of the insecurity of this flux. But the "me" exists only through identification with what it imagines it has been and wants to be. The "me" is "a mass of contradictions, desires, pursuits, fulfillments and frustrations, with sorrow outweighing joy." One source of sorrow is the constant mental conflict between "what is" and "what should be." The conditioned mind, in Krishnamurti's analysis, flees from the facts of its impermanence, its emptiness, and its sorrow. It builds walls of habit and repetition, and pursued its dreams of the future or clings to that which has been. These defenses paralyze us. They keep us from living in the present moment.

Krishnamurti objects to methods of meditation, the solution so many others advocate. While the mind may try to escape from conditioning through meditation, Krishnamurti says, it simply creates in the very attempt another prison of methods to follow and goals to achieve. He opposes techniques of every kind and urges the putting aside of all authority and tradition: From them, one can only collect more knowledge, while understanding is needed instead. According to Krishnamurti, no technique can free the mind, for any effort by the mind only weaves another net. He, for example, emphatically opposes concentration methods (quoted in Coleman, 1971: p. 114):

> By repeating Amen or *Om* or Coca-Cola indefinitely you obviously have a certain experience because by repetition the mind becomes quiet . . . It is one of the favorite gambits of some teachers of meditation to insist on their pupils learning concentration, that is, fixing the mind on one thought and driving out all other thoughts. This is a most stupid, ugly thing, which any schoolboy can do because he is forced to.

The "meditation" Krishnamurti advocates has no system, least of all "repetition and imitation." He proposes as both means and end a "choiceless awareness," the "experiencing of what is without naming." This state is beyond thought; all thought, he says, belongs to the past, and meditation is always in the present. To be in the present, the mind must relinquish the habits acquired out of the urge to be secure; "its gods and virtues must be given back to the society which bred them." One must let go all thought and all imagining. Advises Krishnamurti (1962: pp. 8–10):

> Let the mind be empty, and not filled with the things of the mind. Then there is only meditation, and not a meditator who is meditating . . . the mind caught in imagination can only breed delusions. The mind must be clear, without movement, and in the light of that clarity the timeless is revealed.

Krishnamurti seems to advocate an end state only, a methodless method. But on closer scrutiny, he directly tells all who might hear the "how," while at the same time he insists that "there is no how; no method." He instructs us "just to be aware of all this . . . of your own habits, responses." His means is constantly watching one's own awareness. Krishnamurti's "nontechnique" is more clear from his instructions to a group of young Indian schoolchildren. He first told them to sit still with eyes closed and then to watch the progression of their thoughts. He urged them to continue this exercise at other times, including when walking or in bed at night:

> You have to watch, as you watch a lizard going by, walking across the wall, seeing all its four feet, how it sticks to the wall, you have to watch it, and as you watch, you see all the movements, the delicacy of its movements. So in the same way, watch your thinking, do not correct it, do not suppress it—do not say it is too hard—just watch it, now, this morning.

He calls this careful attention "self-knowledge." Its essence is "to perceive the ways of your own mind" so that the mind is "free to be still." When the mind is still, one understands. The key to understanding is "attention without the word, the name." He instructs, "Look and be simple": Where there is attention without reactive thought, reality is.

The process Krishnamurti proposes for self-knowledge duplicates mindfulness training. But Krishnamurti himself would most likely not condone this comparison because of the danger he sees inherent in seeking any goal through a technique. The process he suggests for stilling the mind springs spontaneously from the realization of one's predicament, for to know "that you have been asleep is already an awakened state." This truth, he insists, acts on the mind, setting it free. Krishnamurti (1962: p. 60) assures us:

> When the mind realizes the totality of its own conditioning . . . then all its movements come to an end: It is completely still, without any desire, without any compulsion, without any motive . . .

This awakening is for Krishnamurti an automatic process. The mind discovers, rather, is caught up in, the solution "through the very intensity of the question itself." This realization cannot be sought: "It comes uninvited." Should one somehow experience the realization of which Krishnamurti speaks, he assures us that a new state would emerge. In this state, one is freed from conditioned habits of perception and cognition, devoid of self. To be in this state, says Krishnamurti, is to love: "Where the self is, love is not." This state brings an "aloneness beyond loneliness" in which there is no movement within the mind, rather a pure experiencing, "attention without motive." One is free from envy, ambition, and the desire for power, and loves with compassion. Here feeling is knowing, in a state of total attention with no watcher. Living in the eternal present, one ceases collecting impressions or experiences; the past dies for one at each moment. With this choiceless awareness, one is free to be simple; as Krishnamurti (Coleman, 1971: p. 95) puts it:

> Be far away, far away from the world of chaos and misery, live in it, untouched . . . The meditative mind is unrelated to the past and to the future and yet is sanely capable of living with clarity and reason.

PART THREE

MEDITATION PATHS:
THEIR ESSENTIAL UNITY

IN SOME respects, every method of meditation is like all
others, like some others, and like no other. The first level
is that of the most general commonalities, disregarding
the idiosyncratic variations of technique, emphasis, or
belief of any one system. At this most universal level, all
meditation systems are variations on a single process for
transforming consciousness. The core elements of this
process are found in every system, and its specifics un-
dercut ostensible differences among the various schools
of meditation.

15. PREPARATION FOR MEDITATION

There is the least common ground among meditation systems on the preparatory groundwork the meditator
requires. The systems surveyed here represent the full

spectrum of attitudes toward the meditator's need to prepare himself through some kind of purification. They range from the emphatic insistence on purification as a prelude to meditation voiced in the Bhakti, Kabbalist, Christian, and Sufi traditions to the views of Gurdjieff and Krishnamurti that such efforts are pointless if they entail avoiding normal life situations. Finally, there is the notion among, for example, TM and Zen schools that genuine purity arises spontaneously as a by-product of meditation itself. Tantrics of the Bon Marg mark an extreme attitude toward purity in advocating the violation of sexual and other proprieties as part of spiritual practice.

Ideas about the best setting for meditation likewise cover a full spectrum. The Desert Fathers withdrew into the Egyptian wilderness to avoid the marketplace and worldly company; hermetic solitude was essential to their program of severe self-discipline. Modern Indian yogis seek out isolated mountains and jungle retreats for the same reasons. Westernized versions of Indian yoga such as TM, however, oppose any forced change in the meditator's living habits; instead, meditation is simply inserted into an otherwise normal daily agenda. Intensive Zen practice is done ideally in a monastic setting, but, like TM, it can be part of a meditator's normal daily round. Both Gurdjieff and Krishnamurti are emphatic that the settings of family, work, and the marketplace are the best context for inner discipline, providing the raw material for meditation.

In most classical meditation systems, however, a monastery or ashram is the optimal environment for meditation, monks or yogis the ideal companions, the role of the renunciate the highest calling, and scriptures the best reading. Modern systems such as TM direct the student to organizational ties and activities while he lives his ordinary life style without imposing any major change. Krishnamurti stands alone among spiritual spokesmen in not advocating that the aspirant seek out the company of others on the same path, just as he objects to the aspirant's looking for guidance from a teacher or master—essential elements in every other system.

In propagating no explicit doctrine, Krishnamurti is again unique. Though other schools such as Zen de-emphasize intellectual study, they all have both formal and informal teachings that students assimilate. In some traditions, formal study is a major emphasis: The Benedictine monk, for example, is to spend one-third of his day in study, the other two-thirds in prayer (or meditation) and manual labor.

16. ATTENTION

The strongest agreement among meditation schools is on the importance of retraining attention. All these systems can be broadly categorized in terms of the major strategies for retraining attention described in the Visuddhimagga: concentration or mindfulness. By using the Visuddhimagga map as an example, we can see similarities of technique obscured by the overlay of jargon and ideology.

The differing names used among meditation systems to describe one and the same way and destination are legion. Sometimes the same term is used in special but very different technical senses by various schools. What translates into the English word "void," for example, is used by Indian yogis to refer to jhana states and by Mahayana Buddhists to signify the realization of the essential emptiness of all phenomenon. The former usage denotes a mental state devoid of contents (e.g., the formless jhanas); the latter refers to the voidness of phenomenon. Another example: Phillip Kapleau (1967) distinguishes between zazen and meditation, saying that the two "are not to be confused"; Krishnamurti (1962) says only "choiceless awareness" is really meditation. The recognition that both zazen and choiceless awareness are insight techniques allows one to see that these seemingly unrelated remarks are actually emphasizing the same distinction: that between concentration and insight. By "meditation," Kapleau means concentration, while Krishnamurti denies that concentration practices are within the province of meditation at all.

Table 2 classifies techniques from each meditation system according to the Visuddhimagga typology. The criterion for classification is the mechanics of technique: (a) *concentration*, in which mind focuses on a fixed mental object; (b) *mindfulness*, in which mind observes itself; or (c) both operations present in *integrated* combination.

A second prerequisite for classification is internal consistency in descriptions. If it is a concentration technique, other characteristics of the jhana path are mentioned—for example, increasingly subtle bliss accompanying deepened concentration or loss of sense-consciousness. If it is an insight technique, other characteristics of insight practices, such as the realization of the impersonality of mental processes, must be present. If a combined technique, both concentration techniques as well as insight must be mixed and integrated, as in Theravadan vipassana.

TABLE 2
AN APPLIED ATTENTIONAL TYPOLOGY
OF MEDITATION TECHNIQUES

System	Technique	Type
Bhakti	Japa	Concentration
Kabbalah	Kavvanah	Concentration
Hesychasm	Prayer of the Heart	Concentration
Sufi	Zikr	Concentration
Raja Yoga	Samadhi	Concentration
Transcendental Meditation	Transcendental Meditation	Concentration
Kundalini yoga	Siddha yoga	Concentration
Tibetan Buddhism	Vipassana	Integrated
Zen	Zazen	Integrated
Gurdjieff	Self-remembering	Mindfulness
Krishnamurti	Self-knowledge	Mindfulness
Theravada	Vipassana	Integrated

In concentration, the meditator's attentional strategy is to fix his focus on a single percept, constantly bringing back his wandering mind to this object. Some instructions for doing so emphasize an active assertion of the meditator's will to stick with the target percept and resist any wandering. Others suggest a passive mode of simply regenerating the target percept when it is lost in the flow of awareness. Thus, an ancient Theravadan text exhorts the meditator to grit his teeth, clench his fists, and work up a sweat, struggling to keep his mind fixed on the movements of his respiration; a TM meditator, on the other hand, is told "easily start the mantra" each time he notices his mind has wandered. Though these approaches are opposite on a continuum of activity-passivity, they are equivalent means to constantly reorient to a *single object* of concentration and so develop one-pointedness. With mindfulness techniques—whether Gurdjieff's "self-remembering," Krishnamurti's "self-knowledge," or zazen's "shikan-taza"—the attentional fundamentals are identical: They all entail continuous, full watchfulness of each successive moment, a global vigilance to the meditator's chain of awareness.

There are perhaps few pure types among meditation schools, save for those systems centered around a single technique, for example, TM or Krishnamurti. Most schools are eclectic, using a variety of techniques from both approaches. They make allowances for individual needs, tailoring techniques to the student's progress. Sufis, for example, mainly use the zikr, a concentration practice, but also at times employ insight techniques like *Muragaba*, which is attention to the flow of one's own awareness. For simplicity, in the preceding sections a specific technique has been emphasized, generally the main one.

Different meditation systems may espouse wholly contradictory views from each other on the necessity for virtually every preparatory act, be it a specific environment, the need for a teacher, or prior knowledge of what to expect from meditation. But the need for the meditator to retrain his attention, whether through concentration or mindfulness, is the single invariant ingredient in the recipe for altering consciousness of every meditation system.

17. SEEING WHAT
    YOU BELIEVE

The meditator's beliefs determine how he interprets and labels his meditation experiences. When a Sufi enters a state in which he is no longer aware of his senses, and his only thought is that of Allah, he knows this to be fana; when a yogi is no longer aware of his senses, and his mind is totally focused on his deity, then he will say he has entered samadhi. Many different names are used to describe one and the same experience: jhana, samyana or samadhi, fana, Daat, turiya, the great fixation, and transcendental consciousness. All seem to refer to a single state with identical characteristics. These many terms for a single state come from Theravadan Buddhism, raja yoga, Sufism, Kabbalah, kundalini yoga, Zen, and TM, respectively.

The history of religion is rife with instances of a transcendental experience interpreted in terms of assumptions specific to time, place, and belief. The Indian saint Ramana Maharshi saw his own transcendental states in terms of Advait philosophy. He conjectures that during Saul's great experience on the Damascus road, when he returned to normal consciousness, he interpreted what happened in terms of Christ and the Christians because at the time he was preoccupied with them (Chadwick, 1966). A person's reference group gives him a gloss on his inner realities; Berger and Luckmann (1967) point out that while "Saul may have become Paul in the aloneness of religious ecstasy . . . he could *remain* Paul only in the context of the Christian community that recognized him as such and confirmed the 'new being' in which he now located this identity."

The interaction among the meditator's beliefs, his internal state, and his self-definition is made clear by a recent example drawn from kundalini yoga. In this tradition, the guru is crucial to the meditator both in helping him achieve sought-after meditation states and in interpreting and confirming the significance of these same experiences.

Swami Rudrananda, a teacher of kundalini yoga, describes the incident that preceded his being awarded the rank of swami. While he was meditating, his master touched him on the shoulder, at which point (Rudi, 1973: p. 85):

I immediately felt within me a surge of great spiritual force which hurled me against the stone walls and allowed a great electric shock to send a spasm of contortions through my body. Movements similar to those of an epileptic controlled my body for about an hour. Many strange visions appeared and I felt things opening within me that had never been opened before.

Rudrananda took his experience to confirm his worthiness of the title "swami," an advanced status. While a set of beliefs about altered states in meditation may render them safe, the meditator does not need specific foreknowledge of these states to experience them. In his autobiography (1972), for example, Swami Muktananda tells how his guru would assign him a meditation practice but give no further hints as to what to expect beyond the barest instructions. When Muktananda subsequently entered extraordinary states, he did so naively. Only after undergoing these states did he chance upon books that gave him an interpretive framework for understanding what had happened. Sri Aurobindo's biographer, Satprem (1970: p. 256), likewise describes the unusual states Aurobindo experienced in the course of his spiritual development but notes:

> . . . Sri Aurobindo was the first to be baffled by his own experience and . . . it took him some years to understand exactly what had happened. We have described the . . . experience . . . as though the stages had been linked very carefully, each with its explanatory label, but the explanations came long afterwards, at that moment he had no guiding landmarks.

18. ALTERED STATES
IN MEDITATION

In meditation, method is the seed of the goal: The contours of the state the meditator reaches depend on how he arrived. The concentrative path leads the meditator to merge with his meditation subject in jhana and then to transcend it. As he reaches deeper levels, the bliss becomes more compelling, yet more subtle. In the way of mindfulness, the meditator's mind witnesses its own workings, and he comes to perceive increasingly finer segments of his stream of thought. As his perception sharpens, he becomes increasingly detached from what he witnesses, finally turning away from all awareness in the nirvanic state. In this state, there is no experience whatever.

Every system that uses concentration describes the

same journey into jhana, though different schools cast the descriptions in differing terms. The key attributes of this state are always the same: loss of sense awareness, one-pointed attention to one object to the exclusion of all other thoughts, and sublimely rapturous feelings. Systems that use mindfulness describe the path of insight: increasingly finer perception of the meditator's mind, detachment from these events, and a compelling focus on the present moment. The nirvanic state, per se, is not necessarily cited as the end point of this progression.

These two altered states are the prototypical altered states in meditation. They do not, however, exhaust all the possible changes in consciousness that meditation brings. Attention is extremely flexible and can change awareness in many more ways than the two major ones described here. Attentional retraining can also be linked with exercises in other biosystems, for example, with movement in Sufi dancing. Additional practices such as controlled respiration, fasting, visualizations, or adopting strong beliefs all contribute to the final shape of the altered state, over and above the effects of the meditator's attentional exercises.

Attention is the key to meditative altered states, but the addition of other practices compounds the complexity of the calculus of the resulting changes in awareness. One example of a more complex altered state is that produced by the kundalini yoga technique of shaktipat-diksha. The seizurelike activity in this state may be due to breath-control exercises as well as to expectations arising from the intense guru-student relationship, and perhaps in part to modeling—all in addition to the basic effects of concentration. The more means used to alter consciousness, the more intricate the topography of the resulting state.

The literature of every meditation system describes an

altered state. Jhana is the prototype of one variety, in which the altered state is a neatly delimited enclave of awareness set off from other states. Jhanic states are mutually exclusive of the normal major states: waking, sleeping, and dreaming. Another type of altered state, however, merges with these major states. This merger appends new functions on the normal states, changing their character. This meets Tart's (1971) criterion for "higher states of consciousness": (1) all functions of "lower" states are available, that is, waking, sleeping, and dreaming; and (2) some new aspects, derivative of an altered state, are present in addition. This kind of transmutation of awareness is an altered *trait* of consciousness, an enduring change transforming the meditator's every moment. The "awakened" state is the ideal type of an altered trait of consciousness. Virtually every system of meditation recognizes the awakened state as the ultimate goal of meditation (Table 3).

In TM, for example, "transcendental consciousness" is the altered state that infuses normal states. The stages ensuing after "transcendental consciousness" from further evolution are "cosmic consciousness," "God consciousness," and finally, "unity." Each represents a deeper infusion of meditative awareness into normal states. Most systems agree that such altered traits occur gradually and to differing degrees. In the Visuddhimagga, for example, there is a similar gradient in the four levels of purification arising from increasingly deep penetration of the nirvanic state.

The goal of all meditation paths, whatever their ideology, source, or methods, is to transform the meditator's consciousness. In the process, the meditator dies to his past self and is reborn to a new level of experience.

TABLE 3

NAMES FOR THE AWAKENED STATE

System	Name of Awakened State
Bhakti	Sahaj samadhi
Kabbalah	Devekut
Hesychasm	Purity of heart
Sufi	Baqa
Raja Yoga	Sahaj samadhi; jivamukti
Transcendental Meditation	Cosmic consciousness; God-consciousness; unity
Kundalini Yoga	Turiyatita; Siddha
Tibetan Buddhism	Boddhisattva
Zen	Mujodo no taigeu ("no-mind")
Gurdjieff	Objective consciousness
Krishnamurti	Choiceless awareness
Theravadan Buddhism	Arahantship

Whether through concentration in jhana or through insight in nirvana, the altered states the meditator gains are dramatic in their discontinuity with his normal states. But the ultimate transformation for the meditator is a new state still: the awakened state, which mixes with and recreates his normal consciousness.

Each path labels this end state differently. But no matter how diverse the names, these paths all propose the same basic formula in an alchemy of the self: the diffusion of the effects of meditation into the meditator's waking, dreaming, and sleep states. At the outset, this diffusion requires the meditator's effort. As he progresses, it becomes easier for him to maintain prolonged meditative awareness in the midst of his other activities. As the states produced by his meditation meld with his waking activity, the awakened state ripens. When it reaches full maturity, it lastingly changes his consciousness, transforming his experience of himself and of his universe.

Though sources like the Visuddhimagga draw distinctions according to the angle of entrance to this transformation (concentration or insight), it is likely that at this point all paths merge. Or, more to the point, from our perspective the similarities may far outweigh the differences. An awakened being transcends his own origins; persons of any faith can recognize him as exceptional or "perfect," or—if so inclined—revere him as a saint.

BIBLIOGRAPHY

ABU AL-NAJIB. *A Sufi Rule for Novices.* M. Milson (trans.). Cambridge, Mass.: Harvard University Press, 1975.

AMMA. *Dhyan-yoga and Kundalini Yoga.* Ganeshpuri, India: Shree Gurudev Ashram, 1969.

ANANDA MAYEE MA. *Matri Vani.* Gurupriya Devi (ed.). Varanasi, India: Shree Anandashram, 1972.

ARBERRY, A. J. *Sufism: An Account of the Mystics of Islam.* London: Allen & Unwin, 1972.

BENNETT, J. G. *Gurdjieff: Making a New World.* London: Turnstone Books, 1973.

BERGER, P. L. and T. LUCKMANN. *The Social Construction of Reality.* New York: Doubleday, 1967.

BHARATI, AGEHANANDA. *The Tantric Tradition.* Garden City, N.Y.: Anchor Books, Doubleday, 1970.

BHIKKU SOMA. *The Way of Mindfulness.* Colombo, Ceylon: Vajirama, 1949.

BLOFELD, J. *The Zen Teaching of Hui Hai.* London: Rider, 1962.

BUTLER, D. C. *Western Mysticism.* New York: Harper, 1966.

CHADWICK, A. W. *A Sadhu's Reminiscences of Ramana Maharshi.* Tiruvannamalai, India: Sri Ramanasram, 1966.

CHANG, G. C. C. *The Hundred Thousand Songs of Milarepa.* New York: Harper Colophon Books, 1970.

CHOGYAM TRUNGPA. *Cutting Through Spiritual Materialism.* Berkeley: Shambala, 1975.

————. *The Myth of Freedom.* Berkeley: Shambala, 1976.

COLEMAN, J. E. *The Quiet Mind.* London: Rider & Co., 1971.

CONZE, F. *Buddhist Meditation.* London: Allen & Unwin, 1956.

DALAI LAMA, THE FOURTEENTH. *An Introduction to Buddhism.* New Delhi, India: Tibet House, 1965.

DOGEN. *A Primer of Soto Zen.* Honolulu: University of Hawaii Press, 1971.

DOYLE, L. J. (trans.). *St. Benedict's Rule for Monasteries.* Collegeville, Minnesota: The Liturgical Press, 1948.

ELIADE, M. *Yoga: Immortality and Freedom.* Princeton, N.J.: Princeton University Press, 1970.

EVANS-WENTZ, W. Y. *Tibetan Yoga and Secret Doctrines.* London: Oxford University Press, 1968.

————. *The Tibetan Book of the Great Liberation.* London: Oxford University Press, 1969.

FRENCH, R. M. (transl.). *The Way of the Pilgrim.* New York: Seabury Press, 1970.

GOVINDA, LAMA ANAGARIKA. *The Psychological Attitude of Early Buddhist Philosophy.* London: Rider, 1969.

GUENTHER, H. V., and CHOGYAM TRUNGPA. *The Dawn of Tantra.* Berkeley: Shambala, 1975.

GURDJIEFF, G. I. *The Herald of Coming Good.* New York: Samuel Weiser, 1971.

HALEVI, Z'EV BEN SHIMON. *The Way of Kabbalah.* New York: Samuel Weiser, 1976.

KABIR (R. Tagore, transl.). *Poems of Kabir.* Calcutta: Macmillan, 1970.

KADLOUBOVSKY, E., and PALMER, G. E. H. *Early Fathers from the Philokalia.* London: Faber & Faber, 1969.

————. *Writings from the Philokalia on Prayer of the Heart.* London: Faber & Faber, 1971.

KALU RIMPOCHE. *The Foundation of Buddhist Meditation.* Dharamsala, India: Library of Tibetan Works and Archives, 1974.

KAPLEAU, P. *The Three Pillars of Zen.* Boston: Beacon Press, 1967.

KASHYAP, J. *The Abhidamma Philosophy.* Vol. I. Nalanda, India: Buddha Vihara, 1954.

KRISHNAMURTI, J. (D. Rajagopal, ed.). *Commentaries on Living.* Third series. London: Victor Gollancz, 1962.

LAO TZU. *Tao Te Ching.* D. C. Lau (trans.) Baltimore: Penguin, 1963.

LEDI SAYADAW. *The Manuals of Buddhism.* Rangoon, Burma: Union Buddha Sasana Council, 1965.

————. *Gospel of Sri Ramakrishna.* Mylapore, India: Sri Ramakrishna Math, 1928.

MAHARISHI MAHESH YOGI. *On the Bhagavad Gita.* Baltimore, Md.: Penguin Books, 1969.

————. *The Science of Being and the Art of Living.* Los Angeles: SRM Publications, 1966.

MAHASI SAYADAW (Nyanaponika Thera, transl.). *The Process of Insight.* Kandy, Ceylon: The Forest Hermitage, 1965.

————. *Buddhist Meditation and Its Forty Subjects.* Buddha-gaya, India: International Meditation Center, 1970.

MAHATHERA, P. V. *Buddhist Meditation in Theory and Practice.* Colombo, Ceylon: Gunaseca, 1962.

MARMION, REV. D. COLUMBA. *Christ the Ideal of the Monk.* St. Louis: Herder, 1926.

MEHER BABA. *Discourses I, II, III.* San Francisco: Sufism Reoriented, 1967.

MERTON, T. *The Wisdom of the Desert.* New York: New Directions, 1960.

————. *The Way of Chuang Tzu.* London: Allen & Unwin, 1965.

MIURA, I. and SASAKI, R. F. *The Zen Koan.* New York: Harcourt, Brace & World, 1965.

MUKTANANDA PARAMAHANSA, SWAMI. *Soham-japa.* New Delhi: Siddha Yoga Dham, 1969.

————. *Gurukripa.* Ganeshpuri, India: Shree Gurudev Ashram, 1970.

————. *Guruvani Magazine.* Ganeshpuri, India: Shree Gurudev Ashram, 1971.

————. *Guru.* New York: Harper & Row, 1972.

NANAMOLI THERA. *Mindfulness of Breathing.* Kandy, Ceylon: Buddhist Publication Society, 1964.

————. *Visuddhimagga: The Path of Purification.* Berkeley: Shambala, 1976.

NARADA THERA. *A Manual of Abhidhamma, I & II.* Colombo, Ceylon: Vajirarama, 1956.

NICHOLSON, R. A. *Studies in Islamic Mysticism.* Cambridge: Cambridge University Press, 1929.

NYANAPONIKA THERA. *Abhidhamma Studies.* Colombo, Ceylon: Frewin, 1949.

————. *The Heart of Buddhist Meditation.* London: Rider, 1962.

————. *The Power of Mindfulness.* Kandy, Ceylon: Buddhist Publication Society, 1968.

NYANATILOKA MAHATHERA. *The Word of the Buddha*. Colombo, Ceylon: Buddha Publishing Committee, 1952 (a).

———. *Path to Deliverance*. Colombo, Ceylon: Buddha Sahitya Sabha, 1952 (b).

———. *Buddhist Dictionary: Manual of Buddhist Terms and Doctrines*. Colombo, Ceylon: Frewin & Co., 1972.

OUSPENSKY, P. D. *The Fourth Way*. New York: Vintage, 1971.

PODDAR, H. P. *The Divine Name and Its Practice*. Gorakhpur, India: Gita Press, 1965.

PRABHAVANANDA, SWAMI, and ISHERWOOD, C. *How to Know God: Yoga Aphorisms of Patanjali*. New York: Signet, 1969.

RAMANA MAHARSHI. *Maharshi's Gospel, I & II*. Tiruvannamalai, India: Sri Ramanasram, 1962.

RICE, C. *The Persian Sufis*. London: Allen & Unwin, 1964.

RUDI, *Spiritual Cannibalism*. New York: Quick Fox, 1973.

SARADANANDA, SWAMI. *Ramakrishna the Great Master*. Mylapore, India: Sri Ramakrishna Math, 1963.

SATPREM (Tehmi, transl.). *Sri Aurobindo: The Adventure of Consciousness*. Pondicherry, India: Sri Aurobindo Society, 1970.

SCHOLEM, G. *Kabbalah*. New York: Quadrangle/The New York Times Book Co., 1974.

SHAH, I. *Wisdom of the Idiots*. New York: Dutton, 1971.

———. *The Sufis*. New York: Doubleday, 1972.

Srimad Bhagavatam. Gorakhpur, India: Gita Press, 1969.

SUZUKI, D. T. *The Zen Doctrine of No-Mind*. London: Rider, 1949.

———. *Essays in Zen Buddhism (second series)*. London: Rider, 1958.

———. *The Field of Zen*. New York: Harper & Row, 1970.

TART, C. "Scientific Foundations for the Study of Altered States of Consciousness." *Journal of Transpersonal Psychology 3:* 93–124, 1971.

VIVEKANANDA, SWAMI. *Bhakti-yoga*. Calcutta: Advaita Ashrama, 1964.

———. *Raja-yoga*. Calcutta: Advaita Ashrama, 1970.

VYAS DEV, SWAMI. *First Steps to Higher Yoga*. Gangotri, India: Yoga Niketan Trust, 1970.

WADDELL. *The Desert Fathers*. Ann Arbor, Michigan: University of Michigan Press, 1957.

WALKER, K. *A Study of Gurdjieff's Teaching*. London: Jonathan Cape, 1969.

WEI WU WEI. *Posthumous Pieces*. Hong Kong: Hong Kong University Press, 1968.

INDEX